Biography

Dr. RUDOLPH R.WINDSOR was born in Long Branch, New Jersey. After living in a number of Jersey communities, his family settled in Philadelphia where he attended Community College, studying Psychology and Political Science. He continued his educational pursuits at Gratz College majoring in Hebrew/Aramaic Studies, Temple University where he majored in Middle Eastern Studies, and the University of Metaphysics where he received his Ph.D. in metaphysical philosophy.

In addition, he is married to Mary L. (Robinson) Windsor and has four sons and a daughter.

He says of his book, "My motive in writing it is to give the true history of the Afro-Americans, which has been excluded from some textbooks." Dr. Windsor is a strong advocate of the economic, cultural and moral development of the black community. In serving the community, he has been a member and president of several organizations, was a delegate to the Black Power Conference of 1968, and a delegate on behalf of the Ethiopian Jews to meet with Mr. Makonen, an official of the Ethiopian Mission to the United Nations in the early 1970's.

Moreover, Mr. Windsor is the author of the book: The *Valley of the Dry Bones* and three other titles. After much consideration, he established his own company called Windsor Golden Series, and in 1988 Mr. Windsor redesigned the cover of his first book *From Babylon to Timbuktu.*

Finally, Dr. Windsor, over the years, has appeared on radio and TV talk shows—lectured at congregations—organizations, universities, and has traveled to Europe, the Middle East, Africa, and the Caribbean.

The author wish to thank the Jewish People for their great effort in assisting the Ethiopian Jews.If you would like to help,write to:Ameri-Association For Ethiopi-an Jews 2028 "P" Street, N.W. Washington,D. C. 20036.

Falasha Bar Mitzvah: *May 1984, Ashkelon—Seventeen Ethiopian Jewish children who recently came to Israel and three Doral boys celebrated their Bar Mitzvah at Jeshurun Grammar School in Ashkelon. Each child received a hand calculator provided by the AAEJ, who arranged for the event. Pictured are Murray Greenfield (left), Israeli Representative of the AAEJ, and Shlomo Bahash (right), Principal.*

BENEFIT DINNER HONORS GRAENUM AND EMMA BERGER

Congressman Stephen J. Solarz (D-NY) (left), guest speaker at the dinner, presented Dr. and Mrs. Berger with a Congressional letter of commendation.

Last November, Graenum and Emma Berger were honored by friends, family, and the AAEJ at a special tribute dinner commemorating their thirty years of tireless activity on behalf of Ethiopian Jewry. As founding president of the AAEJ, Dr. Berger brought the plight of this endangered Jewish community to the attention of Jews and Jewish leaders in North America and Israel. His efforts, both here and abroad, helped to bring about the rescue of thousands of Ethiopian Jews. Today, Dr. Berger continues to strive and to persist in his struggle, and in so doing, to save more lives.

At the dinner, Congressman Stephen J. Solarz (D-NY), the guest speaker, presented the Bergers with a Congressional

A MESSAGE FROM ED ASNER

Photo: Michael Jacobs

This year, if a tragedy is to be prevented, then immediate and dramatic steps must be taken to save the 7,000 Jews left behind in Ethiopia's Gondar province. Unless they are brought to Israel soon, their survival will continue to be threatened by famine, drought, and the proximity of the bloody civil war in nearby Tigre and Eritrea. In addition, due to the absence of decent medical care, at any time, a single epidemic could claim many Jewish lives. Just recently, an outbreak of typhus occurred in southern Gondar.

In November 1984, I sent an urgent message to the delegates at the Council of

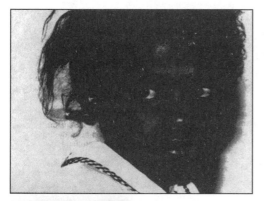

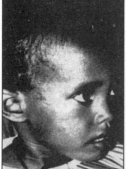

Ethiopian Jewish Children *in the Absorption Center in Pardis Hannah.*

NUMBER	NAME	MEANING	OLD HEBREW	SQUARE	CURSIVE	RASHI	OLD GREEK	LATIN
1	ALEPH	ox		א			A	A
2	BET	house		ב			B	B
3	GIMEL	camel		ג			Γ	C
4	DALET	door		ד			Δ	D
5	HE			ה			E	E
6	VAV	hook, nail		ו			Y	F
7	ZAYIN	weapon		ז			I Z	G
8	HET	window		ח			θ	H
9	TET			ט				
10	YOD	hand		י			K	I
11	KAPH	palm, hand		כ			K	K
12	LAMED	goad		ל			Λ	L
13	MEM	water		מ			M	M
14	NUN	fish		נ			N	N
15	SAMEKH	fish? support		ס			Ξ	
16	AYIN	eye, well		ע			O	O
17	PE	mouth		פ			Π	P
18	TZADE			צ				
19	QOPH			ק			Φ	Q
20	RESH	head		ר			P	R
21	SHIN	tooth		ש				S
22	TAV	sign, cross		ת			T	T

Ashdod, Israel—Four Generations of an Ethiopian Jewish Family *gathered last week at a Seder here to celebrate the Festival of Freedom and the simultaneous arrival from Ethiopia of great-grandmother Zanuba Bayena (seated fourth from left) on the eve of Passover. The 78-year-old Falasha reached Israel from Ethiopia with the assistance of the AAEJ. She joined two sons, a granddaughter, five grandchildren, a two-year-old Sabra great grandson, and other family members. Seated with his baby, Gideon, (named for the last Falasha "King of the Jews") is Rahamin Elazar, 27, a recent graduate of Tel Aviv University and secretary of the government-sponsored Public Committee for Ethiopian Jews. Also pictured are Rahamin's brother Joseph, 25, (on his left) and their mother Ouda Elazar, 59 (on Joseph's left). Several nephews are also seen at the Seder table, celebrating this unique Passover Festival of Freedom.*

Julie Schulman worked as an AAEJ student volunteer in Israel last summer. She is pictured here with some of her new friends at Kiryat Gat.

FROM BABYLON TO TIMBUKTU

FROM BABYLON TO TIMBUKTU

*A History of the Ancient Black Races
Including the Black Hebrews*

by Rudolph R. Windsor

WINDSOR'S GOLDEN SERIES
P. O. Box 310393
Atlanta, Georgia 30331

First Edition
1969 by Rudolph R. Windsor (hardback)
Second Printing, 1973
Third Printing, 1976
Fourth Printing, 1978
Fifth Printing, 1880
Sixth Printing, 1982 (paperback)
Seventh Printing, 1983
Eighth Printing, 1985
Ninth Printing, 1986
First revised and reprint edition 1988 by
Windsor Golden Series
(paperback and hardback
Eleventh Printing, 1990
Twelfth Printing, 1991
Thirteenth Printing, 1993
Fourteenth Printing, 1995
Fifteenth Printing, 1997
Sixteenth Printing, 1999
Seventeenth Printing, 2000
Eighteenth Printing, 2001
Nineteenth Printing, 2003

Library of Congress Catalog Card Number: 70-82729
ISBN 0-9620881-1-0 (paperback)
Printed in the Unites States of America

Dedicated to my mother, Leatta Jones, who worked so hard to rear her five children and who encouraged me in the writing of this book.

Preface

This book is intended as a supplement to existing literature on African and black Hebrew history. To get a background knowledge of the history of the black races, the reader is urged to start at the beginning and continue to the end. The aim is to present material that will not only inform and interest the reader but will impart truth, self-confidence, and racial pride to the black man, and at the same time enlighten the general public concerning the contributions to civilization of the ancient black races.

In general, I have tried to follow a chronological approach in the book, but it has been difficult to maintain a one hundred per cent consistency. Certain subjects are to some extent repeated because I have elsewhere dealt with another phase of the same material. In many cases a refresher is provided in order to bring the reader up to date.

I have consulted many scholars in the compilation of this work. Basil Davidson is an authority on African history; moreover, Allen H. Godbey and Joseph Williams are excellent scholars on the black Hebrews, but I have not hesitated to differ from them in some instances.

It behooves me to express my debt to the faculty of Gratz College who taught me much, and helped make this book possible. Among these are such distinguished scholars as Dr. Elazar Goelman (Dean), Daniel Isaacman (Registrar), Dr. William Chomsky, Dr. Samuel Pitlik, Dr. Samuel Kurland, Dr. Sidney M. Fish, Dr. Esra Shereshevsky, Dr. Samuel T. Lachs, Abraham Marthan, Rabbi Shlomo Balter, and Rabbi Shlomo Margalit. I also want to express my gratitude to my family, uncles, and friends who gave me much encouragement.

RUDOLPH R. WINDSOR

Contents

FROM BABYLON TO TIMBUKTU

CHAPTER I

Ancient Black Civilization

More than six thousand years ago in the land called Mesopotamia there developed the most remarkable civilization then known to mankind. This civilization was centered between the Tigris and the Euphrates rivers. These rivers begin in the mountains of Armenia and flow in a southeastern direction toward the Persian Gulf. The soil of this area is tremendously fertile because of the alluvial deposits brought down by the two rivers. European civilization developed from ancient black civilization. Without this black civilization, white domination and influence as we know it today would have been improbable.

A number of different tribes were entrenched in the southern part of the Tigris-Euphrates region. This southern section was known at different times by many names, among which are Sumer, Akkad (or Accad) and Chaldea; but the name best known to us is Babylonia. This area was also the location of the Garden of Eden, and the people of this region were jet black.[1]

I shall prove conclusively that the black people have the most ancient history of all humans. The best available source of proof is the history of the Jews, known as the Bible. In Genesis 2:10 it is written: "And a river went out of Eden to water the garden; and from thence it was parted and became into four heads." There were four rivers which watered the Garden of Eden. I shall cite the third and the fourth rivers first; then I shall proceed to the first and the second rivers, because it fits better into my line of reasoning. Genesis 2:14 reads: "And the name of the third river is Hiddekel: that is it which goeth toward the east of Assyria. And the fourth river is Euphrates." Commentators and scholars have identified the river Hiddekel; they say it is the Tigris River.[2] Now I shall cite Genesis 2:13. "And the name of the second river is Gihon: the same is it that compasseth the whole land of Ethiopia."[3] Because the Garden of Eden is associated with the land of Ethiopia, we can conclude that the people were black. Rashi, the eleventh-century commentator on the Bible, said that the Gihon is the Nile River that bows through eastern Africa. Rashi, most likely, makes this point because the Nile flows in Ethiopia and into Egypt.

Dr. Speiser, who was a professor at the University of Pennsylvania, said: "There is . . . no basis for the detouring of the Gihon to Ethiopia [he meant the Ethiopia in Africa], not to mention the Pishon in various remote regions of the world." I agree with Dr. Speiser that we should not search for the Gihon in Africa, nor the Pishon in a remote area of the earth; but that we should search for the Pishon and the Gihon in the Tigris-Euphrates valley. There were two Ethiopian nations in ancient times (eastern Ethiopia and western Ethiopia). This point Dr. Speiser failed to elucidate, possibly because of an oversight. There was an Ethiopian civilization in southern Mesopotamia (Babylon), but the people in this region did not use their tribal name, Ethiopia, to designate their nationality. They called themselves by the name of the cities that they constructed and inhabited, or they called themselves by an event that happened there; for example, God confused the language of the people at the Tower of Babel (Babel means confusion in Hebrew). This is why the Ethiopian tribes called themselves Babylonians, referring to the name of the city that they constructed.

There are many nations that are not designated by their true nationality; for example, the white Australians came from England, but those Englishman who live in Australia do not call themselves by their ancestral name.[4] They call themselves by the name of the country which they colonized, which is Australia. The people of Australia are represented in the United Nations by the name of their nation (Australia) and not under their ancestral name, England.

The people who resided in the lower part of the Tigris-Euphrates valley were Ethiopian, black in complexion. We read in Genesis 10:8 that "Cush begat Nimrod; . . . " The word Cush means Ethiopia, and Cush was the father of the Ethiopians. For the meaning of the word Cush, see *Webster's New Collegiate Dictionary*. Nimrod was a mighty Ethiopian conqueror and builder in the land of Shinar.[5] We find in Genesis 10:8-10, that Nimrod ruled over such cities as: Babylon, Erech, Accad (or Akkad); all these cities are situated in the land of Shinar. Another name for Shinar is Sumer.[6] This civilization was of a high order, and one of the oldest civilizations in ancient times. In Genesis 10:7 we read: "And the sons of Cush; Seba and Havilah, . . . " Now we have learned that Havilah was the son of Cush, who was an Ethiopian. The word Havilah became the name of a tribe and a region, known as the Land of Havilah[7] and the Havilites (Ethiopians) lived in the Land of Havilah; moreover, scholars have located this land near the Persian Gulf. In search of the Land of Havilah, we find that there was another Havilah who was one of the sons of Joktan (read Genesis 10:26-29); but this Havilah was of the line of Shem, read Genesis 10:22. Noah had three sons: Shem, Ham, and Japheth. The children of Shem are called Shemites. The sons of Ham are called Hamites, and the sons of Japheth are called Japhites. We should not confuse Havilah, the son of Joktan, with Havilah, the son of Cush. Now it is logical to conclude that Havilah, the son of Cush, is intended in Genesis 2:11 to be the Havilah of the Land of Havilah; because that Havilah[8] was a Cushite (Ethiopian), his habitation would naturally be adjacent to his brother, Nimrod, who ruled Babylon.

Abraham was one of the fathers of the twelve tribes of Israel; and Abraham's father (Terah) came from the land of Ur of the Chaldees, Genesis 11:26-28. The Land of Ur of the Chaldees was located at the southern part of the Euphrates. The Chaldeans were one of many Cushite tribes. Cush means black, according to the Bible dictionary. This dictionary defines further: "Cush, the name of a son of Ham, apparently the eldest; and of a territory or territories occupied by his descendants. The Cushites appeared to have spread along tracts extending from the higher Nile to the Euphrates and the Tigris rivers. History affords many connections between Babylon, Arabia, and Ethiopia."[9] There is more than adequate evidence that the ancient nations of Babylon, Akkadia, Sumer, the Chaldea were inhabited by Cushite tribes (Ethiopians), on all sides of the Tigris and Euphrates rivers.

The Pishon and the Gihon rivers mentioned in Genesis 2:11-13, wind and turn through the Land of Havilah, somewhere near the Persian Gulf. Although it is difficult to identify these two rivers exactly, most likely the center of the Garden of Eden was in the lower part of the Tigris-Euphrates valley. This was the most fertile region in the Middle East, with its many canals and lakes. No wonder it was called the Garden of Eden.[10] It was so well watered that the vegetation looked better than an English park. The Tigris and Euphrates rivers join before they reach the Persian Gulf; then they separate again, making four rivers of the channels of these two rivers. This is one of the theories of the top rated authorities.[11]

The modern names of the rivers that flow into the Tigris and Euphrates are: The Great Zab (south of Nineveh), the Little Zab (south of the Great Zab); the Diyala River flows into the Tigris at Baghdad, Iraq.

SUMER AND KISH

Before the dispersal of mankind at the "Tower of Babel," this region was not called Babylon. It was only after the confusion of the language and the dispersal of the people, that the name Babel was given to the Tower. This conclusion is reached by way of logic. What was the name of this region and Tower before the confusion of the language and the dispersal? *Webster's Dictionary* (gazetteer section) says Sumer is the southern division of ancient Babylon. Moreover, this same dictionary says on page 849, Sumerian: "the pre-Semitic population of the lower Euphrates Valley." The "pre-Semitic population" means that the black Sumerians were there first. This point is in harmony with my original position that the people in lower Mesopotamia were eastern Ethiopians. These Sumerians or Ethiopians and their kindred appear to have settled along tracts from Mesopotamia to India. This area now includes: southern Iran, Afghanistan, Pakistan, and northwest India.[12] The first and second allusions to Sumer in the Bible are in Genesis 10:10, 11:1 under the name Shinar. *Webster's Dictionary* (gazetteer section) hints to this relationship of Shinar and Sumer. There is definitely a blood relationship between the Dravidian tribes of India and the Ethiopian Sumerians. The Sumerian civilization preceded the Babylonian. The Sumerians founded cities that existed more than 4,000 years B.C. such as: Eridu, Lagash, Nippur, Kish, and Ur. Archeologists have found skeletons of ancient Dravidian and Nedda types in Ur and Kish. Antiquated Sumerian statuettes resemble the statuettes of the Dravidian civilization.[13]

CHAPTER II

The Origin of the White Race

After the destruction of mankind by the flood, Noah and his wife, his three sons and their wives were the only people that were saved. (The sons of Noah were Shem, Ham, and Japheth. From these three sons of Noah was the whole earth populated.)[1] The Ark rested on Mt. Ararat.[2] Mt. Ararat was located in the land of Armenia. The words Armenia and Ararat mean high ground.

The entire earth at this time was of one speech and one language. Most of the people dwelled in the plain of Shinar; in Hebrew, the Valley of Shinar. Men began to congregate in the territory and to build a tower up to heaven.[3] The Jewish historian, Flavius Josephus, says: "God also commanded them to send colonies abroad for the thorough peopling of the earth," but the people did not obey God. Now, when man was in the process of building the tower, God disapproved of its construction because it showed a disbelief in His word. The Divine had promised Noah that He would not destroy the earth by water again. Nimrod, the Ethiopian, was the leader of the conspiracy against God. He was a mighty man and a conqueror. He held the people under his dictatorship.[4] When God considered what had been done, He confused men's language and scattered them toward the four directions of the earth.

The sons of Noah were: Shem, Ham, and Japheth.[5] Because the world was populated from these three sons of Noah, it is proper to classify men only according to this classification: Shemites, Hamites, and Japhites; and not Caucasoid, Mongoloid, or Negroid. The latter category is a modern anthropological classification that we will deal with more thoroughly later.

The parts of the earth inhabited by the children of Shem were: parts of the territory of Assyria and Elam (Persia) east of the Tigris River, the eastern part of Syria, and parts of the Arabian peninsula. All the children of Shem were black. This position will be supported by arguments and facts later. The second classification of mankind was the Hamites, who controlled the great centers of civilization in ancient time (4,000 B.C.) soon after the flood. This civilization included the continent of Africa, the land of Canaan (Israel), parts of Arabia, Syria, Phoenicia, Turkey, Babylonia, southern Persia (Iran), East Pakistan, and a large part of India.

The third classification of mankind was the Japhites, from Japheth, who was the youngest son of Noah. The offspring of Japheth occupied the "Isles of the Gentiles,"[6] the shore territories of the Mediterranean Sea in Europe and parts of Asia Minor—whence they dispersed northward over the entire continent of Europe and a great part of Asia.

After Noah's ark rested on the Mountain of Ararat, and the dispersal of the children of men at the "Tower of Babel," Japheth's descendants traveled west, north, and northeast of the Mountain of Ararat and the Caucasus mountains. The Japhites[7] settled near the mountains Taurus and Amanus in Turkey. They journeyed to the river Tanais in southeast Russia, and along Europe to Cadiz (Spain). The sons of Japheth were: Gomer, Magog, Javan, Tubal, Meshech, and Tiras (Gene. 10:2). Gomer was the ancestor of the first Cimmerians and of the later Cimbri, including other offshoots of the Celtic family, and of the present day Gaels of Ireland, Scotland, and the Hebrides Islands. These Cimmerians were described by Homer, the Greek, as dwelling in a remote place of mist and gloom. This place was located north of the Black Sea.

The second son of Japheth was Magog, the father of the Magogites. Flavius Josephus said that the Greeks called these people Scythians. The Scythians included all the wandering tribes who dwelt mostly near the north of the Black and Caspian seas. They were regarded by the ancients as tremendously lacking in intelligence and civilization.

The third son of Japheth was Madai, the father of the Medes. They were located at the southern part of the Caspian Sea; and they later united with the Persians to form one race.

From Javan, the fourth son of Japheth, came the Ionians and all the Greeks.

Tubal, the fifth son of Japheth, is associated with Javan (Isa. 66:19). Meshech and Tubal (Ezek. 32:26 and 39:1) are nations of the north (north of the focal point of the land of Israel). Josephus identified the descendants of Tubal with the early Iberians (Iberes). They were the inhabitants of territory between the Caspian and Euxine seas, which is Georgia in southern Russia. The last son of Japheth was Tiras, the father or ancestor of the Thracians. This land, Thrace, was situated north of Turkey, Asia Minor, and northeast of Greece. Japheth's grandson, Ashkenaz, formed the Germanic race; in the Hebrew language the word means German.

By 378 A.D., the Germanic tribes were on the move. They were known under these names: Lombards, Burgundians, Franks, Saxons, Angles, Jutes, Ostrogoths, Visigoths, Suevis, and Vandals. These ten Germanic barbarian tribes settled all over western Europe, and intermingled with modern nations of western Europe as we know them today. All these tribes were the descendants of Japheth.

The ancient people did not classify races according to skin color, like the modern nations of Europe and America. The ancients, including the Greeks and Romans, identified people according to their national or tribal names. They used such names as Visigoths, Vandals, Saxons, Ethiopians, Carthagians, Jews, Arabs, Persians, Babylonians, Egyptians, and Moors. They did not use the term Negro (which is a modern term) to refer to the black races or the word Caucasian to refer to the white races. Dividing the world along a color line was an idea that originated with the white supremists in Europe after the Renaissance. The Europeans did not have any great civilization immediately after the fall of Greece and Rome.

During the Middle Ages, the black nations of Africa and Asia had the greatest political, economical, educational, and military influence in the world. At this time, Europe existed in a state of darkness for a thousand years. In the seventeenth century and later, Europe began to emerge out of the slough of ignorance, and certain Germans and others conceived of themselves as belonging to a superior race. Johann F. Blumenback, a German (1752-1840), was the first to divide humanity on the basis of skin color. Up to this time, no such attempts had been made. His classification set up a color line, to the detriment of later generations.[8] Mr. Blumenbach classified five chief races of mankind: the Caucasian, the Mongolian, the Ethiopian, the American (American Indians), and Malayan. Moreover, he considered the Caucasian to be the original race.[9] Blumenbach, the anthropologist, named the whites after the Caucasus Mountains (these mountains are situated between the Black and Caspian seas), because he thought the purest white people originated there.[10] Blumenbach was a racist and so was J. A. Gobineau. A third man by the name of H. S. Chamberlain wanted to advance the supremacy of the white Nordic race and its culture.[11] These men attributed psychological value and importance to race. This was racism and it led to a horrible, vicious racial philosophy and to the persecution of the Jews in Nazi Germany.[12] T. R. Garth wrote in his book *Race Psychology* (1931), "Any disposition on our part to withhold from some race the right to a free and full development must be taken as an indication of rationalization on the account of race prejudice, and such an attitude is inexcusable in an intelligent populace."

As I have proven, the earliest civilizations began in

North Africa and the Middle East among the black races.
Read about the black Asiatics in: Herbert Wendt's *It Began
in Babel,* a book on the origin of races (pp. 125-129, and
p. 368).

We have more than adequate proof that the white races
began near the Caucasus Mountains, and from there they
spread north, northwest and northeast into Europe and
Asiatic Russia. Now, we know that the Japhites (Europeans)
are white today. Were they originally white beginning from
their ancestor, Japheth, or did a change materialize in the
skin color of the descendants of Japheth? This question is
difficult to answer. I was told that Japheth was a black man,
but he wanted to be white, so God changed him to a white
man. Evidence to that theory is lacking. Nevertheless, scientists and anthropologists have found different kinds of mutations in certain parts of the world. A physical mutation is a
sudden variation or change, the offspring differing from its
parents in some outstanding characteristic; also a major
change in the chromosomes or genes that determine hered-
ity.[13] Blond hair among the black Australian aborigines is
an example of a mutation;[14] and probably albinos are a good
example of mutations with their white skin, woolly hair,
thick lips, and Ethiopian noses. Any sudden change from
the normal is to be regarded as a mutation. Other examples
of mutations are blondism or whiteness among monkeys,
apes, and chimpanzees.

Major mutations or changes took place among the descendants of Japheth. This is obvious because of their white
skin. In other words, they were black at one time but their
skin changed to white. This phenomenon can be understood
in view of the total world population. Over two-thirds of
the population of the world consists of colored people. That
is a ratio of 2-1. Two out of Noah's three sons remained
black. We know this to be true because many of the people
throughout Africa, Asia, Latin America, and the islands in
the Pacific Ocean are yellow, brown or, black. They have
facial features like the Congoid Africans, especially the Viet-

namese, Filipinos, the people of India (they are a mixture of black Dravidians and Indo-Europeans), Thailanders, Burmese, Indonesians, Guineans, Sumatrans, and the aborigines of Australia, etcetera. You can get a good idea of the features of these people by reading the geographical magazines and observing the foreign students who come from these countries.

There was an Indo-European invasion (Germanic) of the Middle East between the years 2000 and 1500 B.C. These Germanic tribes intermingled with the black people everywhere they traveled. This mingling made the people in Syria, Babylon, Assyria, Persia, India, and parts of Arabia much lighter in complexion. Now, the color of the people in this region ranges from brown to yellow. The Greek and Roman invasions also made these people in the Middle East lighter. Another fact we should not forget is that the Moors and Arabs from North Africa captured and raped European women. As a result, the North Africans became lighter. At one time, these people in North Africa and the Middle East were all black. Whites have intermingled their blood with blacks in Asia, Africa, and the Western Hemisphere. In spite of this, the colored people of the world control about three-fourths of the earth's geographical area. Because the colored people of the world are in a majority, it is proper to infer that the whites have always been a minority, and that the black people are the original people of humanity.

It is interesting and meaningful to learn that the Japhites (Europeans) traveled northwest, north, and northeast of the mountainous region of the Caucasus into Europe. It gives me the impression that the Japhites were isolated, or that they isolated themselves from the civilization and domination of Nimrod, which began in the land of Mesopotamia.

When the Japhites separated at the "Tower of Babel," the theory and probability is that they turned white. There are many cases of individuals turning white in Jewish biblical history. When God wanted to show Moses a miracle, He turned his hand white as snow; then he turned it back

again to its original color (black).[15] In ancient Israel, when
a man had a white spot in his skin, or white or yellow hair,
or white skin somewhat reddish, he was pronounced unclean.[16] All people who were victims of this shameful dis-
ease were isolated outside of the camp or city.[17] Those that
had leprosy were called lepers and they had to shout "unclean, unclean."[18] All people in the ancient world who had
yellow hair and leprosy were despised and segregated. This
is one reason the white supremists discriminate against the
black people today. Miriam and Aaron spoke against Moses
and defamed his character because he married an Ethiopian
woman. As a punishment, God struck Miriam with leprosy
and she turned "white as snow."[19] Now, many people have
deceived themselves in thinking that Miriam and Aaron
spoke against her because she was a black woman; but this
is not the case, because Miriam, Aaron, and Moses were all
black people. They spoke against Moses because the Ethiopian woman was of a different religion. The color issue did
not exist in their day.

To prove this point, the Israelites dwelt among the
Hamites (Canaanites, Hittites, Amorites, Perizzites, Hivites,
and Jebusites). They inter-married. "All the children of
Israel did evil in the sight of the Lord, and served Baalim"
(the idol god). Because they served the idol, Baalim, the God
of Israel became angry and sold them into slavery. It was the
worshiping of the idols, not the marriages that God disapproved. Marriages were forbidden because God feared
that the alien races would persuade the Israelites to worship
their idols; but in Moses' case, he had converted the Ethiopian woman to his religion. Miriam and Aaron used the
Ethiopian woman as an excuse to challenge Moses' authority.
It was a family dispute of jealousy among the three of them.[20]
Moreover, Miriam and Aaron were older than Moses. They
said, "Hath the Lord indeed spoken only by Moses? Hath
He not spoken also by us?" And the Lord heard it.[21] In
another case of leprosy, God showed Moses some miracles to
display to the children of Israel, that they would believe

that Moses was sent by God.[22] In this case Moses' hand turned white.

Naaman and Gehazi had leprosy.[23] I will write a summary of this story: Naaman was the captain of the Syrian army. He acquired leprosy (boils and whitening of the skin). He wanted to be cured. Then he heard about Elisha the prophet. Elisha told him to dip seven times in the Jordan River. Naaman obeyed and he was cured. A reward was offered Elisha, but he refused it. A servant of Elisha, named Gehazi, wanted the reward that his master (Elisha) refused. Then Gehazi ran to look for Naaman. When he found him, he asked him for the reward and said that his master had sent him. This, of course, was a lie. When Gehazi returned to Elisha, Elisha said, "I know you have gotten garments, olive yards and all kinds of wealth by means of subterfuge. Therefore, the leprosy that Naaman had will cleave unto you and unto your seed (descendants) forever"; and he departed from his presence a leper "as white as snow." This type of leprosy affected the reproductive organs (genes and chromosomes that determine hereditary characteristics) in his body. This meant all his children would produce white offspring, even though he was a black man at first. This was the curse of Gehazi.

CHAPTER III

Afro-Asian Culture Goes to Europe

The Sumerians, Babylonians, and Ethiopians were black people. They contributed much to the advancement of civilization. Because they studied astrology, they were capable of formulating many principles of astronomy.[1] These black people[2] were so sagacious and skillful that they were able to divide the years into months, weeks, hours, minutes, and seconds. In mathematics, they developed the decimal system.

The most famous of the Babylonian kings was Hammurabi, who ruled about 2150 B.C. He was outstanding for his codification of a system of laws founded on retaliation as the punitive measure for crime. He also established a seven-day week, with the last day a rest day or Sabbath. This idea was adopted by the Hebrews and then transmitted to the Greeks, Romans, and other Europeans.

The literature of the Babylonians is quite interesting. Long ago these black people wrote with a sharp instrument on clay tablets. Thousands of these tablets have been found; and some of them disclose a popular work known as the Enuma Elish or the Creation Epic. The story of how the world began derived from the Babylonians.

After the dispersal of mankind at the "Tower of Babel," the black Hamites migrated toward the east, south, southwest, and the west.[3] These black Hamites settled in the land of Canaan (later on it was called Israel). The land of Canaan gets its name from the youngest son of Ham,[4] who was

Canaan. The Canaanites were the primordial aborigines of the land of Canaan. We may call them Africans because of their blood relationship to the other inhabitants of the African continent.[5] There were eleven Canaanite tribes living in the land of Canaan and surrounding it before the black Israelites possessed it.[6]

The greatest cultural and commercial cities of these black Canaanites were Tyre and Sidon, sometimes written Zidon. This city gets its name from Sidon, the first-born son of Canaan.[7] The Sidonians and the Tyrians were of the same race, and their kings ruled over both of these cities.[8] In many history books you will read about the Sidonians under the name Phoenicia. The Greeks called the Sidonians Phoenicians (land of palm) because they found many palm trees there; but the Sidonians called their nation by the name of Kenaan (Canaan).[9] Phoenicia, or land of the Sidonians, was located to the north of Palestine, along the coast of the Mediterranean Sea; bounded by that sea on the west, and by the mountain ranges of Lebanon on the east. Tyre and Sidon were founded about 2300 B.C. The Tell-el-Amarna Tablets show that Tyre was a place of great strength in the fifteenth century B.C. Sidon was still older. For a long time it was the only black Phoenician city known to the Greeks. Even after Tyre took the leadership, the Greeks and Hebrews spoke of the Phoenicians as Sidonians, and King Ethbaal of Tyre is called King of the Zidonians.

These black people were proficient in philosophy, astronomy, geometry, arithmetic, and navigation. They had good harbors, which enabled them to navigate to distant lands such as: Cyprus, Sardinia, Crete, Rhodes, Cadiz (in Spain), Sicily, Carthage (in north Africa near Tunis), Tangier, Ophir, and the Canary Isles. These Phoenicians were skilled also in metal work, needle work, and embroidery. They extracted dye from shellfish abounding in the adjacent waters. This dye became known later as Tyrian purple.[10] They made glass from the white sand of the Mediterranean coast.

The Phoenicians spoke a Hamitic-Semitic language so closely allied to the Hebrew that Phoenician and Hebrew, though different dialects, may practically be regarded as the same language. As it was previously stated, there were eleven Canaanite tribes: Sidonians, Hittites, Jebusites, Amorites, Girgasites, Hivites, Arkites, Sinites, Arvadites, Zemarites and the Hamathites.[11] Hebrew has its origin in the Canaanite language.[12] When Abraham came from the region of Babylon into the land of Canaan,[13] he found the Canaanite language similar to his own language. Abraham communicated very well with the inhabitants of the new land, adopted the Canaanite language, made certain modifications, and it became known as Hebrew. The Hebrew language was very similar to the Canaanite says the *Bible Dictionary*.[14] Phoenician or Canaanite can be classified as an African language because the Canaanites were blood brothers of the Egyptians, Ethiopians, Nubians, Sudanese, and other Africans.[15] The Phoenicians established a colony in north Africa called Carthage, and they (the Carthaginians) always considered themselves Canaanites.[16]

When Moses led the black Israelites out of Egypt (northeast Africa), Moses died in the wilderness. Then Joshua led the Israelites into the land of Canaan and dispossessed the Canaanites. Now, it is written in a Jewish book called the Babylonian Talmud:

> For when the Africans came to plead against the Jews before Alexander of Macedon, they said Canaan belongs to us, as it is written, the land of Canaan with the coast thereof; and Canaan was the ancestor of these people (ourselves).

These Canaanites or Africans were driven out of the land of Canaan by Joshua. About 332 B.C. Alexander conquered Palestine. As stated above, the Africans came to Alexander claiming that the land of Canaan belonged to them.[17] The point that I want to elucidate is that these Canaanites considered themselves Africans. Consequently, we can correctly say that the Hebrew-Canaanite language is one of the African languages.

Many of the private houses of these black people were equipped with cisterns for storing water.

The wealth of Phoenicia (or Carthage) was predicated on clandestine, technical procedures in manufacture, secret mines of advantageous and expensive metals, concealed secret trading posts in the remote areas from Ethiopia to the Pillars of Hercules. Their knowledge of navigation enabled them to reach the British Isles[18] and the Arctic Ocean.

The English alphabet derived from two ancient black nations: the Phoenician-Canaanite alphabet and the Hebrew.[19] The Phoenicians had a powerful navy; they were a great trading people. When the Phoenicians traded with the Greeks, the Greeks did not have an alphabet. As a result, they adopted the Phoenician alphabet in order to transact business. The Greeks passed this alphabet to the Romans, and the Romans transmitted it to the German Anglo-Saxon tribes. Then it was brought to the British Isles. The first two letters of the Phoenician and Hebrew alphabet are Aleph and Bet, which is similar to the world alphabet.

The black Phoenicians also gave a system of weights and measures to the Europeans.

The city of Carthage was called the "Queen of the Sea." The Carthaginians controlled the commerce in the Mediterranean Sea. A new nation emerged in the peninsula of Italy (Rome, which challenged the commercial interest and supremacy of Carthage in the Mediterranean. This state of hostility led to three long wars called the Punical Wars.[20] The first Punic War was in the years 264-241 B.C., mostly naval battles which Italy won. The second Punic War was fought in the years 218-201 B.C. A black general by the name of Hannibal was the extraordinary figure who did what was considered the impossible by crossing the Alps with elephants. In Italy he was victorious over the Romans. He was very resourceful and crafty. When he got into a

difficult situation at one time, he drove herds of cattle into
the Romans. His unexpected victories amazed and terrified
the city of Rome. But at the end, because of the lack of men
and supplies, he had to return to Africa (Carthage). The
third Punic War was in the years 149-146 B.C., and fought at
Zama in Africa. Because of Hannibal's skill in warfare, his
strategy is taught in military colleges around the world.

THE EGYPTIANS

The Egyptians are Africans, and descendants of the Hamites. All Hamites are the offspring of their father, Ham.
The first Egyptian was called Mizraim according to the
Hebrews. This Mizraim was the son of Ham (Gen. 10:6).
Ancient and modern scholars have established the location
of Mizraim as Egypt.[21] The word Mizraim is a plural form,
meaning Upper and Lower Egypt.[22]

About thirty-three hundred years before the Christian
Era, Egypt was divided into two kingdoms. A great black
Pharoah (king) named Menes united these two kingdoms
by conquest. The later Pharaohs wore a dynastic insignia
on their crown; the snake of Lower Egypt and the hawk of
Upper Egypt, representing the time when Egypt was divided.
These subsequent Pharaohs held the title of "King of Upper
and Lower Egypt." After Egypt was united, her navy went
out into the Mediterranean and traded with the inhabitants
of the coastal towns and islands such as Crete and Cyprus.

Thousands of years ago, the Egyptians established powerful governments, and built empires that extended in all
directions. They even held dominion over their Canaanite
brothers in Palestine for a long period of time. These black
Egyptians were proficient in mathematics, medicine, engi-
nering, and agriculture. They used geometry to resurvey the
land every year after the Nile River overflowed. Pythagoras,
the Greek mathematician, learned mathematics from the
black Egyptians. By the way, algebra came from the black
Arabs. The word algebra came from the Arabic word *aljebr,*

and it means the science of equations.[23] When the black Moors conquered Spain and Portugal they carried algebra into Europe.

"And Mizraim begat Ludim and Anamim, and Lehabim and Naphtuhim and Pathrusim, and Casluhim—out of whom came Philistim (Philistines) and Caphtorim."[24] When Mizraim begat his children, they dwelled in Egypt; except the Caphtorim and Philistines which inhabited the Island of Crete[25] in the Mediterranean Sea.

In remote ancient times, the people not only of Asia and Africa were black, but also the people of the southern European lands on the Mediterranean Sea.[26] The black races that controlled the commerce and established colonies on the Mediterranean were the Phoenicians and the Philistines. Herbert Wendt, in his book, *It Began in Babel,* says that Crete was a dominant power during and up to the second century B.C. This Cretan power could have been no other than part of the Phoenician-Carthaginian empire, because the city of Carthage did not fall until the year 146 B.C.

Where did European civilization and culture begin? Scholars say that it came from Africa and Asia through Crete. Investigators consider Crete to be the birthplace of European culture. There are many myths surrounding the island of Crete. One is: "It was to Crete that Zeus (father of the gods) abducted the Phoenician princess Europa and there fathered three sons upon her."[27] Zeus came in the form of a white bull and abducted a black princess, because the Phoenicians were a black people. Some scholars believe that before the Indo-European penetration of southern Europe and Asia, Greece was called Europe. Most likely some Cretans settled in Greece.[28]

Herbert Wendt says that the name Europe is derived from the Semitic word *ereb*. He said that the ancient Asiatics considered the word *ereb* to be something dark, ignorant, and mysterious, and therefore, Europe[29] was the dark part of the earth.

A social cataclysm (earthquake) struck the island of Crete

and destroyed its capital at Knossos about 2,000 B.C. These black Philistines migrated from Caphtor (Crete) to the land of Canaan and settled along the southern coast of Palestine. The land of Palestine gets its name from the Philistines who inhabited that region.

CHAPTER IV

The Original Black Jews

Originally all Hamites and Shemites (or Semites) were black.[1] Abraham was a black Shemite and a descendant of Shem.[2] The name of Abraham was Abram before he was referred to as Abraham. The three Hebrew patriarchs were Abraham, Isaac, and Jacob. This Jacob begot twelve sons, who later fathered the twelve tribes of Israel. Abraham was the father not only of the Hebrew-Israelite nation, but also of the Arab nation.

Now, the mother and grandmother of the Arabian nation were black Hamite Egyptian women,[3] and the fathers of the Arabian nation were Abraham and Ishmael (black Shemites). At a certain time, there were hard feelings between Sarah (Abraham's wife) and Hagar, Sarah's maid servant; so Hagar fled from Abraham's house and dwelt in the wilderness. Josephus, the Jewish historian, wrote that Ishmael married an Egyptian woman. As a result, he begat twelve sons:[4] Nebajoth, Kedar, Adbeel, Mibsam, Mishma, Dumah, Massa, Hadar, Tema, Jetur, Naphish, and Kedemah. These twelve sons became twelve tribes and inhabited the region from the Euphrates to the Red Sea in the Arabian peninsula. This country is known today as Arabia. To those who do not believe that the ancient Arabians were black, I would like to make one point crystal clear. If your mother and grandmother were black, I am positive that you would have many colored features.

Abraham, Isaac, Jacob, and the twelve tribes of Israel

were all black people. This I shall prove to you by a gradual method.

After Joseph was sold down into Egypt as a slave, we find in the forty-second chapter of Genesis that he has become the viceroy of Egypt. Joseph's ten brothers came into Egypt (Egypt is in Africa) to buy corn because a famine was in the land. All newcomers who came into Egypt had to buy corn from Joseph; but when Joseph's ten brothers came to Africa they did not recognize him. They did not recognize him because Joseph had grown up and the Egyptians were a black people like the sons of Jacob. Jacob's ten sons considered Joseph to be another black Egyptian. We know this to be true because the ten brothers returned and reported to their father: "The man who is the lord of the land spoke roughly to us. . . . "[5] Furthermore, if Joseph had been white he would have aroused the curiosity of his brothers very rapidly. We really do not need any more proof that the Israelites were black; but for the sake of argument, I will offer it.

In many places in the Bible we find the sons of Jacob and the later Israelites taking black Canaanite women for wives.[6] If the ancient Israelites were not originally black, they would be after the intermingling with black Canaanite men and women.

When the king (Pharoah) of Egypt promulgated an edict to cast all the Hebrew male babies into the Nile River, Miriam and her mother hid the baby Moses in a basket alongside the river. Meanwhile, Pharoah's daughter came down to the Nile to wash herself, and she saw the basket and the baby, Moses. Pharoah's daughter knew that the baby was a Hebrew and she adopted him. If Moses had been a white baby, it would have been difficult to conceal him from her father's anger. In the period of Moses, the black Egyptians enslaved black Jews.

Another point to prove that the Jews were black is the leprosy laws, written in the thirteenth chapter of Leviticus, and explained in the second chapter of this book. The strangest and most amazing phenomena concerning biblical leprosy was that the skin turned white. These laws of leprosy were given to the nation of Israel and they could not apply to a white nation.

Herbert Wendt wrote in his book, *It Began in Babel:* "*All* indications point to the fact that Asia was the cradle of the black race."[7]

It is written in the book of Daniel 7:9: "I beheld till the thrones were cast down, and the Ancient of days did sit, whose garment was white as snow, and the hair of his head like pure wool: his throne was like the fiery flame, and his wheels as burning fire."

The meaning of this verse is as follows: "I beheld till the thrones were cast down." The thrones were placed down and erected. "And the Ancient of days did sit." The God of the universe is the Ancient of days who sat on the throne. "And the hair of his head like pure wool." Daniel saw an anthropomorphic form of God judging the nations in the appearance of a venerable man with woolly hair like a black man. Daniel, the prophet, and the people in his environment (the Babylonians) must have had woolly hair for him to dream of God having woolly hair.

Many Israelites in biblical times intermarried with Canaanite-Hamitic tribes;[8] and if the Jews were not black, the Israelites became much darker (of a surety) after the intermingling.[9]

SUMMARY

There is more than enough evidence to prove that all the original Israelites were black, including the surrounding nations in the Middle East: we must consider the evidence that the Dravidians were the original black people of India; that the Cushites (Ethiopians) inhabited the southern Mesopotamian Valley; that Abraham and Ishmael married African women (Egyptians); that the Canaanites belong to the African family of nations; that ancient Israel intermarried

with these black Canaanite tribes; at the time that Joseph
was viceroy of Egypt his brothers could not distinguish him
from the black Egyptians because Joseph was black; after
Pharaoh promulgated the cruel decree to extirpate the Hebrew males, only a black Moses would have been able to be
concealed effectively for any length of time among black
Egyptians; that Daniel had a dream of an anthropomor-
phous God with woolly hair; that biblical leprosy laws of
the time could apply only to a very dark people with black
hair. The black Jews of India, Abyssinia (Ethiopia), and
West Africa consider themselves the original Jews because
of the purity of their Israelite blood; this has been stated by
Allen H. Godbey.[10]

Now we know that Asia was the birthplace of the black
race. How did these people in Asia become lighter in complexion? There are five answers to this question: (1) The
Indo-European invasion or Germanic invasion of Asia, (2)
The Greek invasion of the Middle East, (3) The Roman
invasion of the Middle East and North Africa, (4) The
Jewish slave trade, and (5) The Arab slave trade. The Indo-
European invaders penetrated the Middle East and mixed
with black Asiatics as far away as India during the second
millennium B.C. The European Scythians passed through
southern Russia and Central Asia as far as the borders of
China.[11] During the Greek and Roman invasions, their
soldiers settled down in the Middle East and North Africa
to disseminate Greek and Roman culture.[12] Moreover, they
married colored women. The Jews sold white slaves[13] to the
Arabs throughout Africa and Asia. When the black Moors
from North Africa conquered Portugal and Spain, they
transported thousands of white slaves of Germanic descent
to Africa.[14] All of these white people who came or were
brought to Africa and Asia were absorbed into the native
population.

BLACK ARABS, BLACK JEWS, AND ETHIOPIANS

Arabia, the land of the offspring of Ishmael, the son of Abraham, is bordered on the east by the Indian Ocean, on the northeast by the Persian Gulf, on the north by the Arabian Desert, and on the west by the Red Sea. The most fertile region of this peninsula is the south and southwest. At one point it almost reaches Ethiopia, which is in Africa. There were many Cushite tribes (Ethiopians) living in the northern,[15] western and southern[16] sections of Arabia. The Arabians have had a long history of intercourse with the Ethiopians in the peninsula of Arabia and with the Ethiopians across the Red Sea in the continent of Africa. James Bruce (author of *Travels to Discover the Source of the Nile*) says that the people in Yemen, Arabia, particularly those of the coast opposite Saba (Sheba), were reputed Abyssinians (Ethiopians) from the earliest periods till after the Moslem conquest.[17] Many of the Arabs are not black today because of the crossing with white slaves in their households and harems.[18]

It is a known fact that there were Ethiopians inhabiting Arabia in the north, southwest, and the southeast. How did these Ethiopians establish domicile (residence) in southwest Arabia? Because Ethiopians lived around the Persian Gulf in northern Arabia, it is highly probable that they migrated toward the southeast and the southwest. It is obvious that the Cushites inhabited vital parts of Arabia before the birth of the progenitors of the Arabs. Raamah, the son of Cush, was the father of the Cushite Sheba and Dedan (Gen. 10:7); about 2300 B.C. The tribe of Raamah became remarkable merchants (Ezek. 27:22). The descendants of Raamah lived in southeast Arabia, and the descendants of Havilah resided in southwest Arabia, which is Yemen. This Havilah was the son of Cush. Moreover, Cush was the patriarch of all the Ethiopian tribes in Babylon, Arabia, India and on the Nile River. The Cushites were residents

of Arabia soon after the confusion of the tongues at Babylon
(2247 B.C.), but Ishmael, the father of the Arabs, was not
born until 1896 B.C. My conclusion is that the Ethiopians
were in Arabia before the Arabs.

In the year 1012 B.C. an Ethiopian queen named Bilkis
visited King Solomon in Jerusalem.[19] Bilkis[20] came from the
Kingdom of Sheba in southern Arabia. Sheba was part of
the Ethiopian empire. This empire included Upper Egypt,
Ethiopia, and parts of Arabia,[21] which included the Kingdom of Sheba. The Jewish historian, Flavius Josephus, calls
this queen the Queen of Egypt and Ethiopia.[22] Calling this
queen the Queen of Ethiopia is proper when you know the
historical background and genealogy of the early inhabitants of Arabia. The Queen of Sheba is known also as the
Queen of the South. The Kingdom of Sheba and Ethiopia[23]
was one empire[24] to the south of the Land of Israel. We must
remember that, on the map, Yemen, Arabia almost touches
Ethiopia in Africa.

It is obvious that the Queen of Sheba had more than
one name, because she is known to the Ethiopians by the
name Makeda.[25] Nevertheless, it is not strange that she had
more than one name. The Ethiopian story of Mekeda, the
Queen of Sheba, is transmitted to us from the Abyssinian
archives. This important document is known as the "Kebra
Nagast" or "honor of the Kings." The Ethiopian account relates the itinerary of the Queen of Ethiopia to meet King
Solomon in Jerusalem. She came with a great train, a retinue
of officials, servants, and abundant wealth. While she was
at Jerusalem, she became infatuated with King Solomon
because of the organization of his affairs, his wealth, his wisdom, his understanding, and physical appearance. Moreover,
the story relates that King Solomon fathered a child by the
Queen of Ethiopia; this child was called David or Menilek
I.[26]

The Queen returned to Sheba (or Saba) with Menilek I.
After Menilek had remained in Ethiopia for some years, his
mother sent him to King Solomon to be educated. Menilek

was crowned King of Ethiopia in Jerusalem, and at that time he accepted the name David. Many experts in the law of Moses, especially one from each tribe, accompanied him to Ethiopia in order to be judges in his kingdom. From these experts, the present Umbares (or supreme judges, three of whom always administer to the King) are said to be descended. In the company of this retinue came also Azarias, the son of Zadok, the former high priest, and brought with him a Hebrew transcript of the law. The present Falashas, the black Jews of Ethiopia, claim descent from those Jews who returned from Jerusalem with Solomon's son, Menilek. Moreover, the present Emperor of Ethiopia, Haile Selassie, claims descent from King Solomon, the Queen of Sheba, and Menilek I. The Queen of Sheba died about 986 B.C. after reigning forty years. Menilek I ascended the thorne, and his posterity, the documents of Ethiopia say, have reigned ever since. James Bruce, the English explorer says, "This is no new doctrine. It has been tenaciously and continuously maintained from the earliest records of the period when all Ethiopia was Jewish; then, in later years, after they had embraced Christianity. Furthemore," says James Bruce, "all the adjacent nations agree with the Ethiopian account, whether adversaries or friends, in regard to the Queen of Sheba. They only differ in the name of the queen." Again this writer says, "All the inhabitants of the coast of Arabia Felix were known as Ethiopians from the most ancient times until after the Islamic conquest. These people were the subjects of the Queen of Ethiopia. They were pagans, then converted to Judaism during the time of the construction of the First Temple; and they were Jews from that time to the year 622 A.D. (as the tradition says), when they became Moslems by the sword of Mohammed."

Before the introduction of the three influential religions in Arabia (Judaism, Christianity, and Mohammedanism), the Arabs worshiped the stars, idols, and the Kaaba stone.

I shall write about the history of the Jews in Arabia. Then I shall write pertaining to the Christians in Arabia;

and last, I shall write concerning the Mohammedans who emerged in the seventh century A.D.

Thousands of Jews migrated to Egypt and Arabia when the Roman general, Titus, destroyed the city of Jerusalem, A.D. 70. When the Jews revolted A.D. 130, Emperor Hadrian dispatched General Julius Severus to Palestine to suppress the revolt. The persecution and restrictions imposed on the Jews were so great that a large number of Jews fled into Arabia. The tradition of the colored Yemenite Jews of Arabia relates that the first Jews came to Arabia with the prophet, Jeremiah, just before Nebuchadnezzar destroyed the First Temple.

In considering the Jews of Arabia, we cannot forget the Jews that accompanied the Queen of Sheba and her son, Menelik I. It is obvious from many indications that the Queen of Sheba or her son, Menelik, transferred[26] their capital from Sheba to Ethiopia in Africa; or that they had a second capital at Aksum, Ethiopia, on the order of a summer residence. It is not exactly known when the capital was transferred or when Aksum came into prominence as a Jewish state, but it probably occurred between the years 990 and 575 B.C. At this last date the Persians conquered Arabia, resulting in the immigration of more Sabaeans and Habashites (Abyssinians) into Ethiopia. Many of the leaders and inhabitants of this Aksumite state became Jewish and seized political domination of ancient Ethiopia, called Aksum. The Aksumite Empire was ruled by Himyaritic immigrants[27] from Arabia, 1st and 2nd centuries A.D. According to tradition, the religious center contained the Ark of the Covenant brought from Jerusalem by the offspring of King Solomon and the Queen of Sheba.

Basil Davidson said that the great period of Ethiopia began soon after A.D. 50 when Aksum became the capital of a new line of kings.[28] It is obvious that these kings were Jews.

The success of trade monopoly in ancient times, on both sides of the Red Sea between Africa and Arabia, meant po-

litical and military control of key harbors. This is the reason
Ethiopia and southern Arabia were included in one empire.
There was much commercial rivalry between Saba (Sheba),
Himyar,[29] Habesh[30] and Aksum that resulted in many wars.
All of the kings and many of the inhabitants of these cities
were Jewish at one time or another. Professor Godbey says
that it is an outstanding point of the tradition going back to
Solomon's time, for both Abyssinia and Yemen, that ancient
Hebrew kings on both sides of the Red Sea had the title
"Bar Negash" or "Sea Kings."[31] The later Himyarite kings,
after 250 B.C., controlled both sides of the Red Sea. When
the prosperous Himyarite kings changed their religion, they
attached the pretext of religious extremism to the reasons
for waging war against their commercial rivals. The Kingdoms of Raidan and Himyar were united against Habesh,
Sheba, and Hadramaut about 500 B.C. The rivalries between
these alliances brought the Roman fleet into military movement in the Arabian Gulf about 1 B.C. to capture the port
of Aden. When the Roman power declined there were Jewish kings in Hadramaut, Sheba, and Yemen continuing the
economic rivalries in trade. During the first, second, third,
fourth, and fifth centuries, Judaism was politically powerful
in Arabia. This power was predicated on trade monopoly.
There were many Jewish kings:[32] Abu Kariba, Masruk, Dhu
Nuwas, etcetera; the most notable was Dhu Nuwas. He will
be taken into greater consideration later.

THE GENESIS OF CHRISTIANITY IN
ETHIOPIA AND ARABIA

About A.D. 329, a group of Tyrians (Phoenicians) were
embarked for India. Their ship met disaster off the shore
of Ethiopia, and the only survivors were the two sons of
the leader. These boys were captured by the Ethiopians and
taken to the court of the king.

Frumentius, one of the boys, became instructor to
Abraha, the prince. Abraha later became king of Ethiopia.

Frumentious taught Christianity to Crown Prince Abraha and others. Frumentius traveled to the Byzantine Empire (Eastern Roman Empire). He had an audience with the temporal head, Constantine the Great, and the ecclesiastical head, St. Athanasius. The leaders of the empire were so tremendously impressed with his abilities that they aided him. Frumentius was promoted to the status of bishop and returned to Ethiopia. The bishop erected and established a church in Ethiopia with the support of the new king, Abraha.

By Abraha's confession of Christianity, he became a Judeo-Christian. He was eager for the spread of his new faith into the land of his ancestors,[33] the Arabian peninsula. Gathering a military expedition of Ethiopians, Abraha crossed the Red Sea with his naval forces and army. He defeated the black Arabs and conquered the pagan city of Mecca after a long siege. After he had introduced Christianity into Arabia, Abraha returned to his capitol at Aksum, Ethiopia.

By the early part of the sixth century A.D. Jewish power in Yemen had reached its zenith. This power was dominant in Yathreb, later called Medina. This was the time of the Golden Age of the black Jews in Yemen, never to be achieved again. These business tycoons maintained international commerce in a multiplicity of commodities with the East and the West; and the Arab converts to Judaism intermarried with the original Jews.

Dhu Nuwas[34] was one of these Arabs who converted to Judaism. He was the king of Yemen about 500 A.D. The Jewish sages were invited to teach Judaism to the people at large. When Dhu Nuwas heard that the Jews were being persecuted in the Byzantine Empire, he retaliated by killing some Byzantine merchants and 20,000 Christians in Arabia. This unwise act brought about the fall of the Jewish kingdom. Judaism was not destined to be disseminated in that manner. "Not by might, not by power, but by my spirit, saith the Lord."

The Christians, in their terrible hour of despair, made an earnest appeal to the Emperor of the Byzantine Empire at Constantinople, but Justinian was hesitant to mobilize a military force because of previous Roman defeats in Arabia. The Emperor was advised by the Abouna (Patriarch) of the Coptic Church in Alexandria, Egypt, to appeal to St. Elesbaan, the Emperor of Ethiopia. St. Elesbaan received the envoys and promised to assist the Christians[35] in Yemen.

St. Elesbaan organized and mobilized an army of more than 65,000 Africans. He appointed one of his most sagacious generals, Abraha, to be his commander. Abraha transnavigated the Red Sea with 150 ships and a large company of elephants. When the two opposing forces confronted each other, the Jews were defeated, and the triumphant Ethiopians marched to Zhafar and captured it.

The Ethiopians ruled over Arabia at this time with an iron hand.

Abraha, the Ethiopian, constructed a marvelous temple at Saana in order to attract the pilgrims (pagan Arabs) who passed through this conquered country on their way to the temple at Mecca. Moreover, Abraha devised outlandish and additional inducements in order to entice the Arabs not to go to Mecca.

One of the Arabs considered Abraha's actions to be an affront to his religion. As a result, he placed dung on the altar of Abraha's temple.

Abraha's reactions were immediate and vigorous to the sacrilege of this pagan Arab. Abraha equipped an army of 41,000 men, horsemen, and armored elephants and marched to Mecca to destroy the temple. Before Abraha reached Mecca, his army was badly battered by a sandstorm. In addition to this, small-pox broke out in his forces. In spite of these difficulties, the general reached Mecca with adequate forces to intimidate the inhabitants of the city. They capitulated and opened the city gates.

When Abraha was riding under the archway of the city gates, his white elephant remained in one spot and would not

move. Because of this, rejoicing broke out among the Arabians. Recognizing an act of God, they assailed the Ethiopians
violently and transformed the history of the world. Abraha
departed from Mecca and died of small-pox and mortifi-
cation.

Because of the obstinacy of Abraha's elephant, the Arabs
have called this period, "The Era of the Elephant," and only
the birth of Mohammed is considered more important.

Soon after this event Mohammed Ibn Abdullah was
born, A.D. 570. He changed the religion of the entire peninsula of Arabia before he died.

THE BIRTH OF ISLAM

At the time of the birth of Mohammed, what were the
international events or conditions operating? The answer to
this question is necessary for a comprehension of the rapid
emergence of the Mohammedan Empire.

The Roman empire, at the birth of Mohammed, was
divided into two parts: The Western Empire with the capital at Rome and the Byzantine Empire with the capital at
Constantinople.

The Roman Empire in the west collapsed A.D. 476 after
many barbarian raids and incursions. The Germanic tribes
crossed the borders and penetrated into all the territory of
the Western Empire, including Africa.[36]

The Eastern Empire was deprived of its vigor by repeated wars with Parthia (Persia). This empire could not
hold its possessions with a firm grip.

Constant imposition of heavy taxes, a scarcity of soldiers
and agricultural laborers, economic exhaustion, a large slave
class, and influx of the barbarians with frequent wars
brought disorder, and weakened both the Western and Eastern Empires.

With the defeat of Jewish and Christian power in Arabia,
the stage was now set for the rise of a new power on the
world scene; this new power was Arabia. The Arabian Em-

pire, with its new religion (Islam), established the super-structure of its culture on the ruins of the Roman Empire in the Middle East, Africa, and parts of Europe.[37]

Europe remained dormant and inactive for a thousand years (through the Dark Ages) while the Moslem Empire mastered the civilized progressive world. Let us return, now, to survey the rise of the Moslem religion and empire in Arabia.

When Mohammed was born many Arabs were still worshiping the sun, stars, spirits, and idols. The Arabs possessed three hundred and sixty idols, one for each day of the year.

Mohammed was born A.D. 570, four years after the death of Emperor Justinian. He was descended from the tribe of Koreish and the family of Hashem. His mentality was prodigious. In his youth he was never taught to read or write,[38] but his imagination was superlative. Mohammed was an extraordinarily handsome man, and eloquent in motivating men with the power of words.

In the early years of Mohammed's life, he passed his time as a shepherd boy. We must remember that many successful men have arisen from insignificant and humble conditions. Watching the sun by day and the stars by night left opportunity for Mohammed to contemplate in solitude, and reflect on the events and profundities of this world.

After Mohammed became a camel-driver, he traveled to remote and intriguing lands. He led his caravans to Persia, Syria, and Egypt, transacting business with merchants of every kind. On his business trips he met Jews, Christians, and members of other sects. He interrogated them concerning the tenets of their religions. He frequented the environment of the Jews and their rabbis, mostly because they were merchants and an omnipresent ethnic group. Because he could not read or write, his ears were attentive and keen to everything that the Jews related to him. Mohammed learned and extracted much from the Jewish religion, and compounded it with his new religion, Islam.

When Kadijah, a rich widow, heard of the good reputation of Mohammed, she employed him in her business. He went on a business deal, transacted it with good results, and returned home at an advantageous time.

Mohammed was amazed at the beauty of Kadijah. He had not seen her before because he had received his position by proxy. Kadijah was immensely gratified by the way he conducted her affairs, and the manner in which he presented himself to her.

Mohammed was not a tall man, but he had such broad shoulders that he looked like a giant. Mohammed had curly black woolly hair that gave him an excellent appearance. Finally, Mohammed married Kadijah, the rich woman of the city of Mecca, when she was about forty years old.

THE FIRST STAGE OF THE ISLAMIC REVOLUTION

According to Alvin L. Bertrand,[39] most mass movements pass through four stages or phases to complete a whole cycle, but Eric Hoffer, the longshoreman, postulates three stages: the vocal stage, the fanatical stage, and the stage of the practical men of action.

Mohammed spent many days in the hills outside of Mecca. He was immersed deeply in the deplorable conditions of his people and he wanted to lead them away from moral turpitude and idolatry. It seemed to him that the angel Gabriel appeared, commissioning him to articulate a new religion to substitute for the old. Incidentally, Gabriel was the same angel who appeared in a vision to the Hebrew prophet, Daniel.[40] Mohammed gradually came to believe that he was a prophet, and expounded his religion to members of his family. He went out to the Holy Temple to preach to the multitudes that gathered to worship the idols. With these words the first phase of the Islamic Revolution began: *La ilaha illa Allah, Mohammed rasul Allah!* (There is no god but Allah, and Mohammed is the prophet of Allah!)

Incidentally, by this time the Hebrew Old Testament had been translated into Arabic, and the Arabs were rapturously pleased to read about their great ancestors in the story of the Hebrew patriarchs.[41] This fact alone helped Mohammed to inspire in the Arabs the feeling of nationalism and racial pride, because they had read in the Hebrew Scripture that Ishmael was to become a "great nation."[42]

Mohammed masterminded the first stage of his revolution by undermining and discrediting prevailing established beliefs and customs and questioning other political, social, and religious institutions. Mohammed attacked the merchants and rulers in Mecca who employed the well of Ishmael and the Kaaba (temple) for monetary gain. Not only did he speak out against idolatry, but also against gambling and drunkenness. Because he spoke against the wine enterprises in the city of Taif, Mohammed was compelled to leave the city.

When Mohammed returned to the city of Mecca, the opposition was intensified against him. A law was enacted that anybody who accepted Islam would be exiled. When the leaders of the city of Mecca were informed that Mohammed was gaining converts in Yathrib, they conspired to assassinate him. This conspiracy motivated Mohammed to flee from Mecca to Yathrib. The night of Mohammed's flight to Yathrib (later called Medina, the city of the prophet) is known as the *Hegira,* the flight.

The Mohammedan Calendar commences with the year of the *Hegira.* It is the most important event in Islamic history. The *Hegira* occurred A.D. 622 when Mohammed was fifty-three years of age.

Coming to Yathrib, Mohammed found the inhabitants very hospitable to him and to his new religion. There were two factors that contributed to this hospitality: (1) There were many influential Jews in Yathrib who were allies with the other Arabs. These Jews had introduced the conception of one God. Moreover, the Arabs were somewhat tolerant of the Jews. (2) on a pilgrimage to the temple in Mecca,

some of Yathrib's best citizens had been converted by the
teachings of Mohammed when he lived in Mecca. Finally,
the pilgrims returned to Yathrib and disseminated their new
religion. These converts could readily accept Islam because
they were influenced to a great extent by the concept of the
one God of the Jews. Eventually, Mohammed was proclaimed ruler of the city, and in his honor, the name of
Yathrib was changed to Medina.

ISLAM AND JUDAISM

The prophet Mohammed adopted many principles and
laws from the Jewish religion:[43] first of all, the basic idea
of monotheism, which is the belief in one God. The Jewish
confession of the unity of God is: *Shma Israel Adonai Elo-
henu Adonai ehad!* (Hear, oh Israel, the Lord our God the
Lord is one!) The Mohammedan slogan is as follows: *La
ilaha illa Allah, Mohammed rasul Allah!* (There is no god
but Allah, and Mohammed is the prophet of Allah!)

Mohammed adopted, also, the main details of the Jewish
Calendar, the Day of Atonement,[44] the Sabbath, much of the
Bible, and narratives from the Medrash, and many points
of the ritual law. Incidentally, the Jews pray three times a
day facing the city of Jerusalem, and the Moslems (true be-
lievers) pray five times a day facing the city of Mecca.

Trying his best, Mohammed sought to convert the Jews
to his new religion, but to no avail. The Jews were adamant
and resistant to change. The high esteem which the Prophet
held for the Jews was transformed to enmity, and instead of
allies, he looked upon them as competitors. Mohammed
needed the confirmation of the influential Jews to validate
his mission, as all upstarts need the backing of someone influential. Mohammed, therefore, turned against the Jews
and became their tormentor.

THE TWO DAUGHTERS OF JUDAISM

The offspring of Judaism are Christianity and Islam. Now history was repeating itself! The proponents of Christianity said to the Jews, we accept your Bible, morals, and monotheism. Only, receive from us Jesus Christ, the great Prophet, the Messiah, of whom all the prophets spoke in the Scripture. Because the Jews refused, they were despised and hated.

Mohammed tried to construct his religion as closely as he could after the Jewish religion. He favored the Jews by accepting many of their laws and traditions. When the Jews refused to be converted, he commanded his followers to stop turning to the Holy City of Jerusalem in prayer, but rather to turn to the city of Mecca. He changed the Jewish Yom Kippur (the Day of Atonement or Fast Day), which he had accepted for the month of Ramadan. Mohammed changed the Jewish Sabbath from Saturday to Friday. We have another parallel with Christianity. In the fourth century, the Church changed the Sabbath to Sunday and reorganized its calendar to make Easter separate of Passover. Like Christianity, also, Mohammed included in his Bible (the Koran) accusations concerning the Jews. Nevertheless, the Koran glorifies many biblical personalities.

In order to win the pagans into the Church, Christianity adopted many barbaric customs and traditions. Likewise Mohammed, to gain the loyalty of the pagan Arabs, adopted many of their beloved customs. The Kaaba Stone (an idol) was to receive high regard in the new religion; also the pagan temple at Mecca was to remain as a holy sight.

THE SECOND STAGE OF THE
ISLAMIC REVOLUTION

The fanatical stage of most revolutions is a bestial, ruthless, bloody, chaotic affair. The throats of men are cut from

"ear to ear." There is an absence of rationalization and
extreme fanaticism sets in.

So it was with Mohammed. He had come to a point of
no return. He became a religious extremist in order to give
his people a better life on a rapid scale. Mohammed came
to the conclusion that all means of persuasion had been ex-
hausted. The period of patience was past and he was now
determined to propagate his religion by the sword. For he
said: "I, last of the prophets, am sent with a sword! The
sword is the key to heaven and hell. All who draw it in the
name of the Faith will be rewarded!" Mohammed became a
martial prophet, and the pagans and stubborn Jews became
his victims.

In the year 627 the Battle of the Foss occurred. The
Jewish tribes were defeated by the armies of Mohammed.
Seven hundred Jews were gathered in the market place and
offered the alternative "the Koran or the sword." But the
devout Jews were accustomed to martyrdom. They did not
hesitate in their choice. Mohammed carried out his bestial
threat, executed the Jews, and the women were sold.

There was another city northeast of Medina called
Chaibar. This city was the headquarters of Jewish power in
Arabia. After a long siege, the city capitulated to Mohammed. Under the rulership of Omar, the Jews of Chaibar
were transplanted to Syria.

Mohammed attacked tribe after tribe and caravan after
caravan that were going to the city of Mecca. These acts
enraged the Meccans and they equipped a large army to destroy Mohammed. In the ensuing battle Mohammed was almost killed. Finally, the prophet marshaled his forces and
entered the city of Mecca. The entire city was abandoned
because its inhabitants were afraid of Mohammed. Mohammed decimated the idols in Mecca. However, he did not
demolish the Temple. When the Meccans saw that Mohammed did not destroy their Temple, they returned to the
city and joined his religion.

The third stage of any revolution is marked by the preservation and continuation of the new order.

The successor of Mohammed was Abu Bekr; he was called Caliph. Abu Bekr wrote down the speeches and sermons of Mohammed. By this time, Islam held a tenacious grip over the lives of the Arabians.

CHAPTER V

Black Civilization in Africa

Before we embark on our voyage into African civilization, I think that it would be interesting to the readers and students of African history to know how the continent of Africa received its name.

First of all, in ancient periods, the black Hebrews referred to Egypt (the guardian of the northeastern gate of Africa) as the Land of Ham.[1] The Hebrew ethnologists used the eponymous name (Ham) because they were conscious of the fact that many of Ham's descendants traveled from Asia toward the south and inhabited the continent we know of today as Africa. It seems that there were no Semites or Indo-Europeans in the Land of Ham (Africa) before the enslavement of the Hebrews and the Hyksos invasion. Ancient Palestine was part of the Land of Ham before the Hebrews came and expelled the Hamitic Canaanites.

It appears that the early anthropologists and ethnologists classified races on the basis of cultural development, and not on the basis of kinship; but the Hebrews are an exception. The early Greeks distinguished between Hellenes and barbarians because they wanted their own people to appear superior. Some of them claim that they originated everything. The advanced Romans felt culturally superior to the northern barbarian tribes, and they enslaved many of these barbarians. The Egyptians subjugated and sold other African tribes that were inferior to them in culture and they conceived of themselves as racially and culturally superior to other underdeveloped people.

The Greek scholars took interest in black people six hundred years after the founding of Naucratis, a Greek colony on the Nile delta. About 1 B.C. the Greek historians Strabo and Diodorus classified the Ethiopian races (black races in the interior of Africa). The Greeks received slaves from the Upper Nile and west of the Nile adjacent to the Ethiopian kingdom. Herbert Wendt[2] quotes Aristotle who says that the pygmies came from the Upper Nile which is Ethiopia. In much of Greek literature, in referring to the African, the Greeks used the word Ethiopian. Moreover, the maps of Africa during the Middle Ages show this continent as Ethiopia. Knowing that the greater part of Africa was called Ethiopia, the professor of zoology and anthropology, Johann F. Blumenbach, classified the human species into five categories, Caucasian, Mongolian, American (Indians), Malayans, and Ethiopians.[3] Notice, the father of modern anthropology does not use the term Negro, but Ethiopian.

But the modern name of this continent is Africa. It is derived from the descendants of Abraham and Keturah. These descendants are Ophren (or Apher)[4] and Japhran. The black Jewish historian, Flavius Josephus,[5] wrote the following: Ophren, the grandson of Abraham through Keturah, led a military expedition against Libya and captured it. When his grandchildren colonized that place, they called it (from his name) Africa.

In the Latin language, the word for Africa is Afer, which is similar to Ophren (or Apher). The *F* in the word Afer and the *Ph* in Apher are interchangeable in many languages.

In North Africa, the Romans won a military victory (the period of the Third Punic War). Ostensibly, the Romans borrowed the word Afer from the ancient Libyans who called their country Apher.

The continent of Africa is a gigantic mass of land. Its

land surface is almost four times larger than the United States.

How and where did Africa receive its black population? Did it come from the south, the east, the north, the west, across the mighty oceans, or did this population originate in the interior of the continent through a gradual process of evolution? Herbert Wendt and Basil Davidson say that it presumably came from Mesopotamia (Babylonia). The history of the ancient black Jews indicates that the early patriarchs of the African people migrated from Babylonia, but there is a proclivity among many scholars to bypass Jewish sources (because of prejudice), and to look elsewhere for the solution in the mythologies of the nations. Much truth has become lost in the worship of many gods and in the deification of many kings.

Can we put any credence in Jewish records that record the ethnology and migrations of the ancestors of the Africans? I think so, because Abraham came from the district of Babylon, which was the cradle of civilization. Abraham had the oral traditions transmitted from Noah and Shem. Abraham rendered obeisance to the one true God; therefore his descendants were able to transmit a long uninterrupted religion, history, culture, and language. No other nation in the ancient Near East can boast or claim as much. Even as great as Egypt was, her ancient religion and language are now extinct.

The Hamites began to arrive in Africa from the Middle East between 5000 and 3500 B.C. These Hamites were (according to the Hebrews): Mizraim (Egypt), Phut (Somaliland and westward) and Cush (Ethiopia). The Hamitic Canaanite-Phoenicians did not colonize north Africa until the ninth century B.C., when they established the city of Carthage at Tunis.

The Egyptians[6] and their descendants are Ludim, Anamim, Lehabim, Naphtuhim, Pathrusim, Casluhim, Philistim, and the Caphtorim. The Naphtuhim settled in the Nile delta and Pathrusim is the city of Pathros in Upper Egypt.

Anamim and Casluhim also settled in various sections of Egypt. But the Lehabim and Ludim occupied the territory west of Egypt now called Libya and on westward. Caphtorim occupied the island of Crete in the Mediterranean Sea, and Philistim eventually inhabited the lower coast of Palestine. When the Israelites under Joshua Ben Nun invaded the Land of Canaan, many of the Hamitic-Canaanite tribes migrated to north Africa.[7]

The Cushites inhabited east Africa along the coast and parts of the interior. More Ethiopians and black Semites crossed the Red Sea from the southern tip of Arabia and traveled into the interior of Africa. The entire continent of Africa was populated from the north and the east. Mary Hastings Bradley, during her journey through Tanganyika, relates a story of the experienced Watusi of Ruanda. She says they have an exact theology—the account of the creation of the world, and a tradition that they came down from the north. Also Hermann Norden[8] writes about the people of Uganda having a legend of crossing the Nile centuries ago. Uganda is south of the Nile and east of the Congo.

The third son of Ham is Phut, sometimes written Put. The descendants of Put have been found in the entire area below the Sahara Desert. They use the names Futa, Foul, Fulas, Poul, Poulbe, and Fulbe. These tribes have dissesminated themselves across Africa from Somaliland to Senegal. Professor Godbey says that they have "prefixed their name to almost every district of any extent which they have ever occupied. They have Futa-Torro near Senegal; Futa-Jallon and Futa-Bondu to the north of Sierra Leone. There is also Futa-Kasson, Futa-Zora, Futa-Ferlo and Futa-Dugu."

EGYPT: THE LAND OF THE NILE

The most extraordinary civilization in ancient times, at the western extremity of the Fertile Crescent, was that of Egypt. What conditions contributed to Egypt's greatness? The factors that made possible the eminence of these black people were the climatic conditions and geography. The conditions that played a great part in the development of Egyptian civilization were the Nile River, a hot climate, an outlet to the Mediterranean Sea and the Red Sea. Egypt is the Nile.

A very peculiar fact about Egypt is that it has little rain. The Nile River runs through this country for about seven hundred and fifty miles from the highlands of Ethiopia, overflowing its banks once a year, during the summer solstice. As the Nile flows toward the Sea, the water brings down alluvial deposits of black earth,[9] making arable land on both sides of the Nile in the Valley. The combination of fertile soil, the Nile as an irrigation canal, interacting with a hot climate, produced for Egypt huge quantities of corn and grain, which helped to feed a growing urban population and large armies. As a result of Egyptian prosperity, we find the ancient Hebrews going down to Egypt to purchase corn. The social scientists know that in order to achieve military expansion, economic development is a prerequisite, and Egypt had solved this problem early in its development.

The yearly flooding of the Nile over its banks contributed a stimulus to learning, especially in astronomy and geometry. The priests wanted to calculate the exact period of the flooding of the Nile. In order to accomplish this, the priests had to observe the heavenly bodies. This involved mathematics and they divided the year into twelve months of thirty days. Our calendar of today is patterned after the Egyptian calendar.

Again, because the Nile overflowed its banks, this event transformed the landmarks of the owners. Real estate had to be resurveyed, lines and angles drawn. This necessity led to the creation of geometry which became, also, necessary in construction, engineering, and warfare.

The Nile played a momentous role, also, as a source of communication and transportation to hold together the union of Upper and Lower Egypt as one autonomous kingdom. The Egyptians of the north could engage in commerce with the south, because strong winds, during most of the year, could push sailboats against the currents.

The concentration of the people around the Nile, was a phenomenon that encouraged ship construction, and stimulated maritime trade with other nations in the Mediterranean Sea; this increased Egypt's naval forces eventually in the Red Sea, and with all of the aforementioned factors operating for Egypt, she became a major power early in her development.

THE OLD KINGDOM

The history of the dynasties in the civilization of Egypt may be divided into three periods. They are as follows: the Old Kingdom or Pyramid Age, the Middle Kingdom, and the New Kingdom or New Empire.

The first king of the First Dynasty of the Old Kingdom was Menes. The date of his accession to the throne was about 3500 B.C. He wore a unique double crown symbolizing the unity of Upper and Lower Egypt. The snake was the symbol in the north, and the hawk was the symbol in the south.

By the time the Third Dynasty arrived, Egypt was well on her way toward greatness (2980-2900 B.C.). The most remarkable king at this time was Zoser. With his power, wealth, and the aid of his counselor, Imhotep, he promoted the city of Memphis, expanded and strengthened the kingdom, built tombs, temples, and terraced pyramids.

During the administration of King Zoser, there lived in Egypt the most phenomenal intellectual of his time. This man was Imhotep, the master. He excelled in many academic pursuits and was preeminent in the field of medicine. J. A. Rogers[10] says that he diagnosed and rendered therapy to more than two hundred various diseases of the human body. The Egyptians practiced auscultation (the listening to sounds in the body), surgery, chemistry, and the recognition of diseases by their characteristics. Imhotep examined the internal and external vital organs of the systemic human body. Furthermore, he investigated the circulatory system.

Herodotus[11] says that the Egyptians were specialists in the medical field and the country swarmed with medical practitioners.

In his day, Imhotep was recognized, also, as a sage, priest, philosopher, poet, scribe, magician, astronomer, and architect.

EGYPTIAN MYTHOLOGY

In the Egyptian pantheon there were many gods. The most famous gods were Osiris, Isis, and Horus. These gods formed a triad. The principal gods were worshiped in a triad; the number three apparently had a mystical importance to the Egyptians. Horus was the son of the sun god (Osiris) and the moon goddess (Isis). The triad was very common in the ancient world and it has come down to our day. Earlier, Osiris was the god of the Nile and Isis represented the god of the earth.

The Egyptians, also, worshiped the animals, nature, and the twelve gods; Hercules[12] was one of these twelve gods. Herodotus, the Greek historian, says that the Greeks adopted the black god (Hercules) from the Egyptians. When the Greeks and Romans took over the gods of Asia and Africa; sometimes they changed their names and color.

Let us return now to our triad, Osiris, Isis, and Horus. I think that more than any other god, the legend of Osiris underwent great transformation through the passage of history. At first, I am certain, he was a subsidiary god, but he arose to the status of a sun god. In Egyptian mythology the legend says Osiris was king of Egypt and he married his sister Isis. When Osiris went off to war, his brother, Set, assassinated him. Set eventually cut the body in fourteen pieces and scattered it over a remote area.

Isis, undespairing, began a search for the fragments and

found them except for the phallus (penis), which had been eaten by a Nile crab.

Isis recomposed the body of her dead husband, skillfully connecting the parts together. She then effectuated the rites of embalmment and this restored the body to eternal life. It was always considered in Egypt that the preservation of the body intact was necessary for the eternal life of the soul. Finally, Isis brought forth a son after the death of her husband. This posthumous birth was "conceived by the union with her husband's dead body, miraculously reanimated by her charms." This mythology reminds one of the spirit entering into the Virgin Mary, thus conceiving the child Jesus.

Afterward, the goddess retreated to the marshland of Buto to flee from the anger of Set, who had usurped the throne, and to rear her son Horus until the day when he would be mature enough to avenge his father's death. According to another version, Set found out that Isis had given birth to Horus. Set entered the swamps in the form of a snake and bit Horus, leaving him on the verge of death. Finally, Isis was told that evil and darkness would persist until Horus was cured.

Many kings of early Egypt were deified, ritually identified in the solar hierachy as the sons of Ra. Ra remained the supreme god, and Osiris, Isis, and Horus, their son were incorporated in the family of Ra, the solar pantheon. Some of the pharaohs were considered in the solar religion to be either the incarnation of Horus the Elder, son of Ra, or the physical son of Ra himself.

The connection of both Osiris and Isis with fertility cults was constantly emphasized from the Empire Age onward, and this encouraged their gradual entry into the realm of the living. Osiris became the leader of this world and the underworld, and his name (in the hieroglyph) from the Twentieth Dynasty onward was the solar disk rather than the eye.

The stories and legends of ancient Egyptian mythology[13]

are voluminous and interesting. They have their counter-
parts in the East and the West, Babylon, Greece, and Rome.
From Greece and Rome, culture and civilization spread over
the entire continent of Europe.

Now, in order to terminate the history of the Old Kingdom, it behooves me to mention the fact that Khufu, the
first king of the Fourth Memphite Dynasty, erected the
largest pyramid. Pepi, the third and greatest king of the
Sixth Dynasty (2590-2570) sent some expeditions against the
Bedouins of Sinai and into Palestine; nevertheless, Egypt
was set for a period of decline. Pepi II reigned 90 years
(2566-2476 B.C.), the longest reign recorded in history; generally an uneventful period of retrogression, with the king
much of the time controlled by a powerful aristocracy. The
Old Kingdom and the first thousand years of recorded history ends with the Eighth Dynasty. This was the beginning
of the period of excessive anarchy. The country was engaged
in a destructive civil war. There was a long wretched period
of disorder. Many potentates claimed the throne at once,
and the cities were in an uproar with widespread confusion.

At this same time, black Hamitic Amorites[14] from the
northern Euphrates River, invaded the Fertile Crescent and
the Egyptian frontier. These Asiatic Amorites, also, penetrated the booming towns of the Nile delta, spreading con-
sternation and panic.

THE MIDDLE KINGDOM

The Middle Kingdom consisted of nine dynasties lasting
for a period of a thousand years. Because of the condition
of anarchy, the need of the hour was for strong leaders. This
leadership was found in the Eleventh and Twelfth Dynasties. Mentuhotep II completed the conquest of the Hera-
cleopolitan Dynasty. The capital of this kingdom was transferred more than three hundred miles south of Memphis to
the city of Thebes. Obviously, the capital was removed to
Thebes so that it would be less subject to attack by Asiatic

invaders. Once again the mighty pharaohs governed Upper and Lower Egypt. When the new kings had restored law, order, and peace, the Egyptians devised more improvements and public works.

Amenemhet III of the Twelfth Dynasty (1849-1801) and other pharaohs established dikes and constructed colossal reservoirs to preserve the water of the Nile for land irrigation. They dug a channel through the land between the Nile delta and the Red Sea. The sophisticated Egyptians excavated canals thousands of years before a French engineer (De Lesseps) dug the Suez Canal A.D. 1869. The ancient Egyptians were meticulous masters in constructional engineering; they were very accurate with the smallest details. Thousands of slaves from all over the known world were forced under harsh regimentation and strict rule to construct temples, monuments, and pyramids for the megalomaniac deified pharaohs.

The Twelfth Dynasty appeared on the international scene as a strongly organized monarchy. The kings had diplomatic relations with remote kingdoms. Sesostris III, fifth king of the dynasty (1887-1849 B.C.), conquered two hundred miles of the Nile Valley up to the second cataract; he established relations with the coast of the Red Sea; he sent military expeditions into the Sinai peninsula and also into Syria. At this time trade was successful on a large scale.

During this Middle Kingdom, Egyptian civilization made its first profound influence on other parts of Africa, such as Nubia, Wawat, Cush, etcetera.

About the time of the reign of Amenemhet IV (1801-1792 B.C.) and the early stages of the Thirteenth Dynasty, Egypt went through a long period of confusion and invasion. The Egyptians were so tremendously disunited that they neglected the defense of the kingdom. It collapsed easily, about 1788 B.C., before a wave of invaders known as Hyksos or Shepherd Kings. These Hyksos dominated Egypt for about two hundred years. This period is known to the Egyptians as the "Great Humiliation."

Now, after long exhaustive investigation, it appears that the Hyksos were descendants of the ancient Horites or Hurrians. A. T. Olmstead[15] confesses that "there is much obscurity about their race. We may at least assert that they were west Semites and that their chief center of power was north Syria." I do not agree with Olmstead when he says they are Semites, however. Much evidence indicates that they are Japhites, Indo-Iranians or Indo-Europeans,[16] descendants of what we call today the white race. But I agree with Olmstead when he says the center of their power was in north Syria. The Hurrians came from the southern parts of the Caucasus Mountains and established their new capital at Mitanni in Syria and Assyria. These Hurrians began to push their way into the black world of the Middle East about 1800 B.C.

Herbert Wendt[17] writes the following: "In ancient Sumerian epics the land of Churrum is mentioned south of the Caucasus, and in the Old Testament the Hurrians appear as the Chori (or Horites). In 1720 B.C. or thereabouts they conquered, under the name of Hyksos, the Kingdom of Egypt where they reigned as Shepherd Kings."

When the Hurrians invaded the Middle East, they were a white or fair-skinned race. They mixed with the indigenous black population, and took up permanent residence among them. Everywhere they traveled they established colonies.

During the second millennium, the Hurrians invaded Egypt under the name Hyksos. They came with horses and chariots, which terrified the Egyptians. The Egyptians had never seen horses before, and the Egyptians probably had never before seen such a heterogeneous population of white, yellow, light-brown, and chocolate people. So the Hyksos came into Egypt and established the Fifteenth and Sixteenth Dynasties. These dynasties are known to the Egyptians as the period of the "Great Humiliation." During this period the Egyptians had to suffer insults to their gods and culture from aliens.

Many scholars think that the Hyksos were in power in

Egypt when the ancient Hebrews came down to live and to purchase corn. This would mean that the Hebrews migrated to Egypt between 1788 and 1580. The Hyksos were hospitable to the Hebrews because they were aliens themselves. It was one of the Hyksos pharaohs who elevated Joseph, the wise Hebrew, to the position of viceroy of Egypt. Because of this, Joseph saved Egypt from starvation.

In the process of time, the Egyptians from the city of Thebes, Upper Egypt, waged wars of liberation against the Hyksos. The new powerful native Egyptian leader advocated an ardent nationalist policy to regain control of the government. As a result, the Hyksos were expelled from Egypt.

THE NEW KINGDOM OR NEW EMPIRE

"Now there arose up a new king over Egypt, which knew not Joseph.

"And he said unto his people, behold, the people of the children of Israel are more and mightier than we.

"Come on, let us deal wisely with them; lest they multiply, and it come to pass, when there falleth out any war, they join also unto our enemies, and fight against us, and so get them up out of the land."

Much proof points to the fact that the new pharaoh who ascended the throne was Ahmose I or Ahmese, the first king of the brilliant Eighteenth Dynasty (1580-1557 B.C.). He re-established the government at Thebes; expelled the Hyksos, and instituted something like a fascist form of government. This government was an autocratic nationalist regime, exercising regimentation of industry, rigid censorship, and forcible suppression of opposition.

The period of ths nationalist dynasty marked a turning point in the fortunes of the Hebrews. They were once well thought of by the overthrown Hyksos Kings. Now they lost their favored status, and their previous contributions to the nation were ignored. Their freedom of movement was restricted, male genocide was decreed, and gradually the Hebrews were reduced to slavery.[18]

"Therefore they did set over them taskmasters to afflict them with their burdens. And they built for Pharaoh treasure cities, Pithom and Raamses.

"But the more they afflicted them, the more they multiplied and grew. And they were grieved because of the children of Israel. . . .

"And they made their lives bitter with hard bondage, in mortar and in brick, and in all manner of service in the field: all their service, wherein they made them serve, was with rigour.

"And the king of Egypt spake to the Hebrew midwives, of which the name of one was Shiphrah, and the name of the other Puah:

"And he said, when ye do the office of a midwife to the Hebrew women, and see them upon the stools, if it be a son, then ye shall kill him: but if it be a daughter, then she shall live."[19]

During the period that the Hebrews were slaves for Pharaoh, they built many of the megalithic structures: the Hebrews erected some pyramids, they dug a great many channels for the river, they built walls for the cities and ramparts, they constructed the halls at Karnak for Thutmose I, they built temple pylons, hypostyle halls and an obelisk for Amenhotep III; by the edict of Ramses II they constructed at Thebes the temple of the Rameseum with its colossal statues of himself, and they built the treasure cities of Pithom and Ramses.

Naturally, the Hebrews were not the only slaves in Egypt. There were Ethiopian slaves, Nubians, Canaanites, Syrians and people from the Aegean Islands; but the Hebrew slaves were in the majority.

The New Kingdom or New Empire Age consisted of the most remarkable and outstanding black personalities known, not only in Egypt, but in the entire civilized world. They were brilliant men possessed with gallantry and the capability to reorganize the civil and military administrations. After the Asiastic invaders had humiliated the Egyptians, the people rapidly forgot their phobias of horses and learned to use chariots. They manufactured sophisticated weapons out of iron. The generals organized horsemen and other soldiers into mighty expeditionary forces to conquer Syria, Mitanni, and the territory extending to the fourth cataract of the Nile.

In the year 1501 B.C. the fourth king of the Eighteenth Dynasty enthroned himself. He was Thutmose III known as the hornet, because he wore this insignia on his crown. Thutmose III was the son of Thutmose I and a concubine, Isis. His qualities of face were pure ink black, a broad nose and thick lips. He reigned jointly with his wife and half-sister, Queen Hatshepsut; ruled alone (1481-1447 B.C.) Thutmose was one of the greatest Egyptian kings. He began his rule by deposing his father in a palace revolution, but with his queen, was temporarily pushed aside by the revolution of Thutmose I (his father) and II (his brother). Eventually, he regained control of the government, invaded Syria with a great army (1479), defeated the king of Kadesh at Megiddo. Thutmose III really lived up to his reputation as the flying hornet. He waged seventeen military campaigns in Asia. His navy conquered the islands of the Aegean Sea and added them to his colossal empire.

IKHNATON OR AMENHOTEP IV

Many years after the death of Thutmose III, a new king called Amenhotep IV became a religious innovator. He was not an excellent soldier or governor. He believed in one god, the sun god Aten, who dominated all living creatures.

Because he was excessively preoccupied with religion, he neglected the kingdom. He ordered that the temples of the old Egyptian gods be closed, and he expelled the priesthood. Also, he changed his name from Amenhotep to Ikh-naton, which means "Aten is satisfied." He transferred his capital from Thebes to Tell el-Amarna.

When Ikhnaton attempted to revolutionize the religion, this act divided the Egyptian aristocracy and weakened the government. Furthermore, Ikhnaton was too busy to send military assistance to the Egyptian allies or to remote countries of the empire which were threatened by revolt or invasion.

FORETELLING OF MOSES

One of the kings of the Eighteenth or Nineteenth Dynas-ties was informed by his astrologer (or sacred scribe) that a child would be born to the Hebrew nation. If he were per-mitted to live, he would bring the Egyptian kingdom to a low condition. The child was born; his name was Moses. He was reared in a miraculous way, in Pharaoh's own palace by his daughter. The plot to destroy Moses in his infancy failed. The daughter of Pharaoh adopted Moses as her son. She came to her father and said, "I have brought up a child who is of a divine form, and of a generous mind; and as I have received him from the bounty of the river, in a wonderful manner, I thought it proper to adopt him for my son, and the heir of thy kingdom." When she put the child into Pharaoh's hand, he hugged the child and put his diadem upon his head. But Moses cast down the diadem to the ground, and, in a childish mood, he twisted it around and stamped upon it. The sacred scribe saw all of this (he was the same astrologer who foretold that Moses' birth would bring down the Egyptian Kingdom). Because of this, the astrologer cried out in a terrifying manner, saying, "This, O King! this child is he of whom god foretold, that if we kill him we shall be in no danger; he himself affords an attesta-tion to the prediction of the same thing, by this trampling upon thy government, and treading upon thy diadem." The astrologer advocated to have Moses executed in order to free the Egyptians from fear and to deprive the Hebrews of hope and freedom. At this intense moment, the daughter of Pharaoh took the child quietly. Because the king loved his daughter, he was not disposed to hurt her. When events arrived at this juncture, the Divine Providence protected Moses, prevailing upon the king to spare him. Moses was educated, as Josephus says, and it is highly probable that he received the best education the ancient world could give. We must remember that Egypt possessed institutions of higher learning and that Pharaoh's palace and temple was the chief center of the educated class. Moses was exposed to the best Egypt had to afford. Those who think Moses was just an ignorant religious leader are quite wrong. Moses knew the political, social, and natural sciences of Egypt: he learned the religious system, the political system, mathematics, geometry, biology, chemistry, anatomy, foreign languages, law, engineering, and military tactics.

Josephus writes the following: "Moses arrived at the age of maturity and he displayed his virtue and abilities to the Egyptians. The Egyptians interpreted Moses' actions as their imminent doom and the elevation of the Hebrews."

During the course of Egyptian history, there were many wars with the Cushite kingdom of Ethiopia (sometimes this region is known as Nubia). When Moses had reached the age of maturity, the Ethiopians were making incursions into Egyptian territory. The Egyptians were in a state of bitter distress because of these predatory attacks. Josephus said that they penetrated as far as the city of Minphis near the Nile delta. Because of the urgency of the military situation, the Egyptians made an inquiry through the oracles and the prophecies. They were told by their god to secure the assistance of Moses. Then Pharaoh commanded his daughter to bring Moses into his presence, but first Pharaoh had to swear to his daughter that no misfortune would happen to him. Moses was brought into Pharaoh's presence, informed of the deteriorating military situation, and given generalship of the Egyptian army. The Egyptian priests gave only tacit approbation to his new assignment; they were skeptical of his loyalty, and hoped that he would be killed in the ensuing battles. The Hebrews were greatly exuberant because of the promotion of Moses. They expected Moses to liberate them.

Moses marshaled his army and marched southward. He did not follow the Nile, but took the inland route, cognizant of the fact that the Ethiopians would be most vigilant at the river. But the land route presented a severe danger. It was inhabited with deadly serpents, which this area produced in mass numbers. Legend says that these snakes fly in the air and descend on men unaware. For that reason, Moses devised an ingenious plan to combat these evil creatures. He filled baskets with an animal called Ibes and transported them along with him. These Ibes are very dangerous to the snake family; they fly after the snakes and consume them completely. When Moses approached the land of the serpents, he let loose the Ibes, and they destroyed the snakes.

Then Moses came upon the Ethiopians secretly; vanqushed them in battle and demolished their cities. Those that escaped retreated to Saba (Sheba), their capital. Josephus says that Saba was a royal city of the Ethiopians which Emperor Cambyses of Persia afterwards renamed Meroe, after his sister. The capital of Ethiopia used to be located at Napata (at the fourth cateract). Later it was moved to Meroe. Moses found the city of Meroe well fortified. It was surrounded by a high wall, and there was a river around the wall that made it look like an island. The city was constructed so strongly that when the water of the river became violent, it could not move the foundation of the city. The city of Meroe was extremely difficult to subdue and the army was lying idle. Then the daughter[20] of the Ethiopian king happened to see Moses as he led the army near the wall, fighting with great gallantry. She finally arranged a treaty of peace with Moses, agreeing to surrender the city if he would marry her. Moses consummated the marriage and departed with his wife for Egypt.[21]

Moses returned to the capital of Egypt during the reign of one of the kings of the Nineteenth Dynasty, probably Ramses I, or Seti I. The Egyptians hated Moses even more when they found out that he was successful in battle. The Egyptians became suspicious of Moses because they thought he would incite a slave insurrection, so they conspired to assassinate him. When Moses learned of the conspiracy he escaped to the land of Midian.

RAMSES II

Ramses II was the fourth king of the Nineteenth Dynasty (1292-1225 B.C.) and the son of Seti I. He was pure black, had thick lips and a broad nose like the people of the western Sudan today. He was a warlike pharaoh, industrious and energetic, ruling Egypt for sixty-seven years. In the early years of his reign, he engaged in the important campaign against the Hittites. At Kadesh, near Syria, the battle was indecisive. Finally, he signed a permanent peace treaty with the king of the Hittites, married the king's daughter; and the remaining years of his life were relatively peaceful.

Ramses II is also known for his national public work projects. Because these projects required the forced labor of thousands of Hebrew slaves, he is known as the Pharaoh of the Oppression. He was a boastful, vainglorious, tyrannical personality who sought to astound humanity by covering the country with megalithic structures. This Ramses transferred the capital to the Nile delta. The black Jews constructed the treasure cities, Pithom and Ramses. Ramses developed the Nile delta and had the slaves build Egypt's megaliths: the colonnade at Luxor and its gigantic pylon, in front of which he placed six colossal statues of himself. Each of these statues was almost sixty feet high. Ramses II erased his predecessors' names from the records and substituted his own. This Ramses also constructed the hypostyle hall at Karnak and the temple called "The Ramesseum" near Thebes.

During this period Egypt enjoyed a high degree of prosperity; a great boom just before the recession. When Merneptah, the son of Ramses II, came to the throne the entire empire was falling apart.

Moses entered Egypt, probably during the reign of Ramses II or Merneptah. He (Moses) was commissioned by the God of Israel to go down into Egypt and to tell Pharaoh to let his people go. Moses did not have any great difficulty entering the palace of Pharaoh; he had been reared in the king's palace, and he knew Egyptian protocol. He decided to enter the palace at the time that Pharaoh was entertaining various ambassadors from foreign nations.

After Egypt was weakened and terrified by the scourge of the ten plagues, Pharaoh agreed to emancipate the Hebrew slaves.

Beginning with the reign of Merneptah and the kings of the Twentieth Dynasty, Egypt was in a state of decline. There were revolts throughout the Empire. It is evident that the emancipation of the Hebrew slaves may have triggered these revolts, producing a chain reaction. Weakness at home and attack from the external enemies marked the defeat and decline of the Empire. In the tenth century B.C., the Libyans invaded Egypt and established the Twenty-second Bubastite Dynasty. Under this Libyan Dynasty, Egypt tried to revive the empire. Sheshonk or Shishak invaded Palestine and entered into combat with the Davidic Dynasty. At this time, most of Shishak's troops were Libyans and Cushites. After two hundred years of Libyan rule, the Cushites invaded Egypt and the Middle East, making themselves a great power. Then the Assyrians, Babylonians, Persians, Greeks, Romans, and Arabs invaded Egypt consecutively, terminating Egyptian rule.

CUSH (ETHIOPIA)

The ancient country of Cush was in the eastern Sudan region of Africa. During the Middle Ages, the Sudan was not united and organized as a single country. The Afro-Asian world considered the Sudan to be that territory extending from the Sahara Desert almost to the Equator, its widest part nearly 1000 miles; also it extended from the Atlantic Ocean to the highlands of Ethiopia in the east, its longest part about 4000 miles. This vast area includes such countries as the modern Sudan, Chad, Niger, Mali, Guinea, Senegal, Gambia, Upper Volta, etcetra. During the colonial period, this area was divided into two parts called the French Sudan in the west and the Anglo-Egyptian Sudan in the east.

The word Sudan is an Arabic word meaning black. The Arabs called this vast area *Bilad es Sudan* (the territory of the black) because the tribes here were very black, unmixed tribes.

In dealing with the kingdom of Cush, we find that it is located in the eastern Sudan near the Red Sea. The country of Cush was situated on both sides of the Nile River between the third and sixth cataracts. The modern nation called the Sudan occupies this territory. The important cities of ancient Cush were Napata, Meroe, Musawarat, Kurru, Kurgas, and Naga. There were two civilizations of the Ethiopian people in the continent of Africa: one was in the highlands of Ethiopia[22] with its capital at Axum; the second was located in the region of the present-day Sudan with its capital at Napata and at other times, at Meroe.

The people in the ancient country of Cush were called Nuba or Nubians as subnames; other subnames they use are Bejas or Bisharin, which are sub-tribes. These people, it would be correct to say, are northern Ethiopians who live in the Sudan. European writers make a practice of calling various tribes in Africa by the infamous name *Negroes*. True Africans are indeed Africans regardless of what they

look like. The Africans have their own tribal names and
they do not need the European appellations of Nigritians,
Negroes, Negrilloes, or Negroids.

CUSHITE CONQUEST

When the power of the Libyan kings of Egypt began
to wane in the eighth century, the northern Ethiopian king,
Piankhi, marched from his capital of Napata and invaded
Egypt. The Cushite kings of Napata and Meroe were sub-
servient to the Egyptian crown for over 1000 years. They
paid tribute mostly in gold, ivory, slaves, cattle, and fighting men. At this time the Ethiopians were brazen enough
to challenge the world's greatest empire. Piankhi's elite
troops and his mighty naval forces attacked city after city
until they reached Memphis. Hermopolis fell before him.
Even the capital of Osorkon III at Heliopolis could not with-
stand his advances. The enemy capitulated at the capital,
and the supremacy of Ethiopia was established in Egypt.

Rogers says that "Piankhi sailed for his home in the
south, his ships laden with silver, gold, copper, clothing,
and everything of the northlands; every product of Syria
and all the sweet woods of God's land. His Majesty sailed
up-stream with a glad heart, the shores on either side were
jubilating. West and East—singing: Oh, mighty ruler
Piankhi, thou comest, having gained the dominion of the
North. . . . "

About 712 B.C. there arose another king (Ethiopian)
over the city of Napata. This new king was called Shabaka
or Sabacon, the brother of Piankhi. He established the
Twenty-fifth (Ethiopian) Dynasty in Egypt. According to
Manetho, he burned Bocchoris alive, the alleged ruler of
the Twenty-fourth Dynasty.

During the long history of the Middle East, there have
always been wars betwen the military powers north of the
land of Israel (by way of Syria) and the military powers
south of Israel (Egypt). Israel was the *betsah bain hapatish*

vehasadan (the egg between the hammer and the anvil). In the time of Ahaz and Hezekiah, the Kings of Judah, Assyria and Egypt were the great powers. Both of these powers had threatened the independence of the little state of Judah, but with the help of God she survived. The prophet Isaiah had told King Ahaz to stand still and do nothing; in other words, Isaiah meant do not make any alliances with Assyria or Egypt, but trust in the God of Israel!

One of the most famous generals of Shebaka was Taharka or Tirhakah, the son of Piankhi. This Ethiopian general advanced against Sennacherib, the king of Assyria, while the Assyrians were threatening the existence of Judah. Taharka captured Philistia in the year 688 B.C., but was defeated at Eltekeh, west of Jerusalem, by the Assyrians. Also Taharka was the third king in the Twenty-fifth Egyptian Dynasty (715-663). At first, he defeated Esarhaddon, but three years later (671) he was expelled from the city of Memphis and never returned.

Ethiopia, this African state, became a great power, even though it was only for a period of a hundred years. If Assyria had not emerged when she did, Ethiopia probably would have lasted another hundred years as a western Mediterranean power. Because the Ethiopians were defeated by the Assyrians, we must not conclude that their existence and influence was stifled or choked out. Indeed, Rogers says that Nastasen, a later king of the Ethiopians, defeated the great Persian conqueror, Cambysis in 525 B.C.

At this time the Ethiopians continued to exercise a political and economic influence over the African tribes to the south and the west. In the same way that culture and civilization spread from Greece and Rome over the entire continent of Europe, in the same manner culture and civilization spread from Egypt and Ethiopia to other parts of the continent of Africa.

It seems that the Cushite civilization developed in two stages, first at the famous city of Napata and second at the industrial city of Meroe. The political power of Napata

was predicated on the affluence of gold. Here is an excellent
description of the abundance of gold in Ethiopia: "Cambyses
thrust his authority far up the Nile, past Thebes and the
first cataract into Ethiopia. This exotic country aroused the
curiosity of the Persians, with its elephants and ivory and
gold. They said that the prisoners in Ethiopia wore fetters
of gold."[23] Ethiopian domination on the Nile began to rise
after the decline of the Libyan kings of Egypt during the
tenth century. Kashta was one of the greatest kings of
Napata; he began the conquest of Egypt which his son
Piankhi continued. The city of Napata was located inside
the river bend between the third and fourth cataracts.

History is witness to the fact that the greatest civilizations developed alongside river banks and so it was with
the Ethiopian cities of Napata and Meroe.

Meroe was a greater city than Napata. It was located between the fifth and sixth cataracts and between the Nile
and the Atbara rivers. Meroe is a very ancient city. As you
have read, Moses, the Hebrew, led an Egyptian army against
it about 1350 B.C. Obviously, it was standing when Thut-
mosis I (1540-1501) established his southern frontier in
Ethiopian territory. This frontier was located past Napata
almost to the fifth cataract. Between 595 and 550 the capital
of Cush was transferred from Napata to Meroe; the primary
motive for this transference was because of the Persian attacks against Ethiopia after 595 B.C. Two other reasons
probably contributed to the removal of the capital: one,
the city of Meroe was surrounded by grassland containing
scattered trees; two, there were large deposits of iron ore
found in this area. The iron ore rendered a great impetus
to the civilization of Cush and other African tribes. L.
Rogers, F. Adams and W. Brown (European writers) state
that: "There is evidence that in the days when Europeans
were still satisfied with rude stone tools, the Africans had
invented the art of smelting iron."[24] Excavators have even
found the furnaces in which the iron ore was smelted, and
they have found mountains of iron slag.

RETENTION OF CUSHITE IDENTITY

Although the Egyptians dominated parts of Ethiopia for over a thousand years, the Ethiopians, to a great extent, maintained their own identity, ideas, and customs. The Cushites were never absorbed (nationally) into the Egyptian social structure. It has been postulated by some authorities that the pharaohs of the Twenty-fifth (Ethiopian) Dynasty accepted Egyptian gods; nevertheless, these kings were interred in their tombs in a position that accorded with Ethiopian tradition, but not according to Egyptian customs. After the year 500 B.C. there emerged a more distinctive Cushite culture, similar to a "Cushite Renaissance." The gods are the gods of Meroe, not Egypt. The stone ram, symbolic of the power of the god Amun, stood outside the temple of Naga, a Cushite city. The Meroites employed the Egyptian hieroglyphic writing in their temple, but after 225 B.C. they devised their own alphabet even before Rome became a great power. They began to create fine pottery with their own original styles. Also they constructed majestic temples and palaces of beautiful design. Many of the ruins of ancient Cush are still standing at Meroe, Musawarat, Naga, and near Napata. Basil Davidson says these sites are waiting for more archeologists (with time and money) to be excavated.

The Cushites built a powerful empire in Africa that extended far and wide. Their political and military sway extended to the Red Sea, to the Axumite kingdom to the south. Evidence has been found that Ethiopian influence extended to Lake Chad and to the Uganda territory. There was even trade with Arabia, India, China, Egypt, Axum, and the neighboring tribes.

Cush was no playboy on the international stage, but was recognized and known among the greatest powers of the day. The Ethiopians fought successive wars with the Egyptians, Hebrews, Assyrians, Persians, and under the

Axumite Kingdom they fought the Arabians. Cush was a
sophisticated power and during her greatness she became
the mistress of the south. The greatness of Ethiopia is written in the annals of the ancient nations; she dispatched her
ambassadors to the known nations of her day. Herodotus,
the Greek historian, knew little about the Ethiopians.
Furthermore, he did not visit this intriguing land. When
Herodotus heard of this land, he called the people *Aithiops;*
in the Greek language this word means burnt face. He never
called them by their national name, which is Cush.

   Finally, the civilization in the highlands of ancient Ethiopia at Axum began to rise. King Ezana of Axum marched
down to the city of Meroe and attacked it, putting an end
to its greatness. The causes of the wars between Meroe and
Axum probably were trade competition and the influx of
Nubians from the Sahara.[25]

THE BLACK AFRICAN HEBREWS OF
EGYPT AND ETHIOPIA

   From what period can we certify the existence of black
Hebrews in Egypt and Ethiopia? It is certain that Israelites
were in Egypt and Ethiopia during the period of King
Takelot of Egypt (Twenty-third Tanite Dynasty about 725
B.C.) and the prophet Isaiah of Jerusalem; because we read
in Isaiah 11:11 that: "And it shall come to pass in that day,
that the Lord shall set his hand again the second time to
recover the remnant of his people, which shall be left, from
Assyria, and from Egypt, and from Pathros [Upper Egypt],
and from Cush [Ethiopia] . . ." In Isaiah 27:13, we get the
understanding that the outcasts of Judah are in the land
of Egypt; in 19:18 the prophet is positive that five cities
(with Jews and Egyptian converts) will accept the God of
Israel and will speak the language of Canaan (Hebrew).
About seventy years after Isaiah, the Prophet Zephaniah
(3:10) says "From beyond the river of Ethiopia my suppliants, even the daughter of my dispersed, shall bring mine

offering." Many authorities have agreed that Zephaniah was speaking concerning the Jews who were dispersed and who colonized the region in and around Ethiopia.

Since the Hebrew prophets and historians, for example Josephus, knew that Jews were in Egypt and Ethiopia, the next question is—what are some of the theories concerning their arrival in these countries? The theories are as follows:

King Solomon married the daughter of the king of Egypt. Obviously, this marriage was for economical and political reasons (I Kings 11:1). Solomon wanted to maintain international peace, security, and commerce. It is probable that he arranged with Pharaoh, his father-in-law, to establish Jewish trade colonies on the Nile River. By the way, Solomon married the daughters of many kings to keep them under his economic and political control.

In I Kings 9:26 we read that "King Solomon made a navy of ships in Ezion-geber[26] which is beside Eloth, on the shore of the Red Sea in the Land of Edom. And Hiram [the King of Tyre or Phoenicia] sent in the navy his servants, shipmen that had knowledge of the sea, with the servants of Solomon. "And they came to Ophir and fetched from thence gold, four hundred and twenty talents, and brought it to King Solomon." Many scholars have postulated that the land of Ophir is on the east coast of Africa, this would be in Ethiopia territory.[27] It would appear highly probable that Solomon would establish trade colonies along the east and west coasts of the Red Sea. Ancient Ethiopia had excessive gold deposits to satisfy Solomon's need. As has been mentioned previously, the Persian troops of Cambyses said, "the prisoners in Ethiopia wore fetters of gold."

The Queen of Sheba visited Solomon: The fact that her visit occurs after the voyage of Solomon-Hiram's navy to Ophir suggests that, in the mind of the writer, Ophir was associated with the territory of that rich Queen of Sheba.

Apparently, when the navy of Solomon came to Ophir, the Queen of Sheba heard about the greatness of Solomon. Josephus,[28] the Jewish historian, certified the fact that the

Queen of Sheba was the Queen of Egypt[29] and Ethiopia.
This would mean that Jewish trade colonies were established
in her territory. Josephus also says that the royal city of the
Ethiopians was Saba[30] (or Sheba—the two words are interchangeable).

According to the Ethiopians and the black Jews of this
country, the Queen of Sheba gave birth to a son of whom
they say Solomon was the father; moreover, they say that
other black Jews accompanied the Queen back to Ethiopia.
The name of the child to whom she gave birth was Menilek.
Years later, as the story is related, Menilek returned to
Jerusalem for his education. On his return trip to Ethiopia,
Solomon sent along with him some leading priests and
officers.[31] All of these events occurred during the tenth century B.C. This was probably the first organized Jewish colony
in Ethiopia.

In this same century, Sheshak, the King of Egypt, invaded Palestine (I Kings 14:25). Without doubt, he must
have transported many Jews to Egypt and Ethiopia because
he took prisoners with him, and his army consisted of
Libyans and Ethiopians.[32] During the late part of the eighth
or the early part of the seventh century, the Ethiopian general Tirhaka invaded Palestine and captured more than a
few towns. The prophet Isaiah certainly knew what he was
talking about when he spoke of the Israelites' exiles in
Tirhakah's country at that time. Even the advance of the
mighty Assyrian army would motivate many Israelites to
take refuge in Egypt, Libya, and Ethiopia. Again, the incursions of the powerful army of King Nebuchadrezzar of
Babylon (in the years 698-675) into Palestine undoubtedly
caused rapid and numerous migratory waves of Israelites
to flee into north and east Africa. In Jeremiah 44:1, the
Prophet addresses the Jews in Egypt and the Jews that live
in Pathros, which is southern Egypt. Jeremiah tells the Jews
(in the eleventh verse) that they are not safe from Nebuchadrezzar. This warning would naturally influence many Jews
to migrate deeper into Ethiopia and the Sahara Desert.

By the time of the Prophet Zephaniah (about 630 B.C.), Ethiopia and the adjacent lands of Uganda and Kenya were swarming with black Jews. Zephaniah says (3:10: "From beyond the rivers of Ethiopia my suppliants, even the daughter of my dispersed shall bring mine offering." This verse is an indication that the Israelites would be multiplying and making converts among the inhabitants beyond the rivers of Ethiopia. No doubt this prophet had communication with the Jews in this remote area.

The "rivers of Ethiopia" connect with the Nile water system in the heart of Ethiopia: the Atbara River extends from the highlands of modern Ethiopia to the Nile; the Blue Nile extends, from the direction of Addis Ababa in a northwestern direction toward the Nile. Near Uganda and the northern Congo is the Bahr el Ghazal River. It is 500 miles long, in southwest Sudan; formed by the confluence of the Bahr el Arab and Jur rivers in northwest Upper Nile; it flows east to unite at Late No with the Bahr el Jebel and form the White Nile. These areas are "beyond the rivers of Ethiopia"; moreover, are there any records or oral traditions of the existence of Jewish tribes deeply "beyond the rivers of Ethiopia"? Joseph J. Williams[33] cites a particular case. He said, "There can be little doubt but that somewhere in the dim past, probably by way of Abyssinia, *a wave of Hebraic culture* penetrated to the Lake District of east Africa," if we may credit the following citations:

Speaking of Uganda to the west of Lake Victoria and northeast of the Belgian Congo; "It has an organized native government, with a tradition of thirty-three kings and a legendary line that traces back to *King David*. It is a proud history. The legends tell of the Uganda people crossing the Nile [remember, beyond the rivers of Ethiopia] centuries upon centuries ago, and subduing all tribes whose country they traversed. They claim the highest native civilization in Africa."

The above report is highly credible in all its details, if we keep in mind what I have written pertaining to the

Egyptian and Cushite Jews. The thing that might be questioned about the Uganda people is not their identity, but the vitality of the Jewishness of their religion.

TABIBAN KAMANT AND WASAMBARA JEWS

Professor Allen S. Godbey[34] says that the word *Tabiban* means smiths; he has located these Jews in central Ethiopia. The Tabiban Jews were really Falashas, but they were forced to accept a nominal Christianity. They were like the Marrano Jews of Spain, forced to accept a religion against their will. The word Falasha in Amharic, the official language of Ethiopia, means immigrants. The Falashas did not call themselves by this name; they used the name "Bet Israel" (the house of Israel), but the Abyssians called them Falashas. Because the other tribes in Ethiopia called the house of Israel Falashas or immigrants, this would suggest that perhaps the Falasha Jews came to Abyssinia at a later date; therefore, they were ostracized because they did not accept Christianity.

The Falashas held the monopoly on the skilled trades in Ethiopia: they were leather-workers, potters, smiths, and masons.

The Kamant Jews were separated into two classes: the Keberti (honored), from these the priests are chosen, and the Yetanti (small or insignificant people). By the way, these two classes were called by names that are similar to the Hebrew. The Kamant Jews esteem Moses highly and many other Old Testament personalities; they observe Yom Kippur and the feasts for the dead. Because they remain isolated from other Jews, Christian, and pagans, they learn very little from the external world.

About thirteen hundred miles south of the territory of the Falashas live the Wasambara people. They are a variety of colors from light brown to black. In their land are found asylum institutions (cities of refuge),[35] they are like the Levitical cities found in the Old Testament. Professor Godbey says, "Taken with sacrifices, wherever Judaism is acknowledged, there must have been introduced by Yemenite or Himyaritic Jewish traders in very ancient times."

Concerning the Wasambara people along the east coast of Africa opposite the Island of Zanzibar we know very little. But it is a known fact among scholars that Jewish merchants from Yemen traded along that coast. It is possible that Jewish colonies were established there at an early date. It is also a probability that Jewish tribes migrated from the north. I have shown previously that Jewish immigrants crossed the Red Sea into Ethiopia and that Jewish immigrants migrated from Egypt to Ethiopia. My conclusion is this: the nation of Ethiopia became a confluence or crossroad of a wave of Hebrew culture and settlements. Here in Ethiopia was the great center of the black Jews; they exchanged ideas, some settled down to stay, others departed to the west and south.

Joseph L. Williams[36] quoting Walter Chicele Plowden, the British Consul in Abyssinia, agrees with my conclusion. After the British Consul reviewed the National records and traditions he concluded: "Two things are certain—that at a far later period, six sovereigns of pure Jewish race and faith reigned at Gondar, and that to this day numerous Jews are found throughout Abyssinia. I think it also highly probable that (at whatever epoch it may be placed) the whole of Abyssinia was of Jewish persuasion previous to its conversion; as even those who have adopted the Christian creed still maintain . . . numerous forms and observances."

As we can conclude from the above and other records, the Christians of Abyssinia were once Jews. Incidentally, Solomon Grazel, in his book *A History of the Jews,* has stated that there still exist 100,000 black Jews in Ethiopia who are not Christians.

After King Abraha of Ethiopia accepted Christianity in the fourth century, A.D., a great change occurred that was disastrous to the existence of the Jews: they became victims of persecution that lasted for many centuries. Ever since the rise of Christianity in Ethiopia, Judaism has been decreasing. Yet in spite of social pressures and discrimination 100,000 black Jews have been able to survve. This multitude of Jews, surviving under hostile conditions, proves their greater numerical strength earlier in their history.

THE JEWS OF THE MALAGASY REPUBLIC

There is an island near the southeastern coast of Africa called the Malagasy Republic; the old name for this island was Madacascar. Near the eastern part of this island on the isle of St. Marie, there exists a group of black Jews who call themselves Zafin Ibrahim, "descendants of Abraham." Professor Allen H. Godbey says that the same alphabetic writing that was present in Palestine about 650 B.C. appeared at the same time in Malaysia. Moreover, he says, since the Hovas of Madagascar are members of the Malayan family who probably immigrated from Cambodia, this indicates the historical connection with the Jews of Madagascar. Like the Jews of Ethiopia, Uganda, and Wasambara, there are a multiplicity of Jewish cultural survivals, complexes, patterns, and traits found functioning among the Jews of Madagascar such as the following: the day counted from sunset to sunset, many fast days, the eating of beef, the New Year festival, the making of a small fire on the first evening of the feast; they have rituals of the purification of the people; they sprinkle blood of the New Year's ritual upon the doorposts. The latter ritual could be reminiscent of the Passover ceremony which is observed in the month of Abiv; this month is the first month of the Jewish civil New Year. In this month the kings of Israel were inaugurated.

THE NORTH AFRICAN BLACK JEWS

In the year 331, that Alexander the Great defeated the Persian emperor, Darius at the Battle of Gaugamela (incorrectly called Arbela) a new master emerged on the world stage and transformed the history and culture of three continents. However, Alexander died in the prime of his life at the age of thirty-two because of debauchery and intoxication. Before the death of Alexander, his desire was to establish a Eurasian state. His scheme was to amalgamate[37] the Greeks with the Asians. This was implemented by the widespread marriage of his troops with the colored women of the east. Most of his troops remained in the subjugated countries and became absorbed into the native population.

After the death of Alexander, his vast empire was divided among his generals. Ptolemy received Egypt and Seleucus received Asia. As time elapsed, there was constant war between these two dynasties. By the year 198 B.C., the descendants of General Seleucus had their capital in Syria, just north of Palestine. In this same year the Seleucid Dynasty in Syria compelled Egypt to give up Palestine, the land of the Jews. The king of Syria at this time was Antiochus III.

When Antiochus IV usurped the throne in Syria (175-163 B.C.), he entertained the thought of uniting Alexander's empire. This meant the conquest of Egypt. However, the province that bordered on Egypt was Palestine, which stood in his way. At this time, the Jews would not accept Greek culture, nevertheless, Antiochus was determined to Hellenize the Jews.

The army of Antiochus marched into Palestine to support Menelaus, the leader of the pro-Syrian party, As a result, many Jews were killed; others escaped to the hills and to Egypt. Only those Jews that supported Antiochus' policies remained in Jerusalem. An edict was promulgated interdicting the observance of the holidays, the Sabbath, and circumcision. A statue of Jupiter was erected in the Holy

Temple above the altar. To this statue the people brought the sacrifices of pig meat, the animal which is an abomination to the Jews. Because of this religious persecution, the legitimate high priest (Onias III) and many other Jews fled into African countries such as Egypt, Ethiopia, and Cyrenaica (Libya). Throughout the last twenty-five hundred years, the main factors that have contributed to the social migration of the Jews were wars, religious persecution, and commerce. All these factors were operating and gave rise to the African Jewish population.

In the year 65 B.C. the Roman armies under General Pompey captured Jerusalem. In 70 A.D. General Vespasian and his son, Titus put an end to the Jewish state, with great slaughter. During the period of the military governors of Palestine, many outrages and atrocities were committed against the residue of the people. During the period from Pompey to Julius, it has been estimated that over 1,000,000 Jews fled into Africa, fleeing from Roman persecution and slavery. The slave markets were full of black Jewish slaves.

> And the Lord shall scatter thee among all people, from the one end of the earth even unto the other; and there thou shalt serve other gods, which neither thou nor thy fathers have known, even wood and stone (Deut. 28:64).

This prophecy and all the residue of the prophecies contained in Deuteronomy 28:15-68 befell the black Jews after they disobeyed the laws of God. Many nations transported the Jews into slavery, and the sons of Israel transmigrated to every continent.

The Jewish philosopher, Philo (about 40 B.C.-40 A.D.), who lived in Alexandria, Egypt, said that one million Jews resided in Libya and Egypt from the Catabathmos to the borders of Ethiopia. Professor A. H. Godbey says that Philo leaves us doubtful about which boundaries of Ethiopia he meant. I think that Philo meant the western and southern boundaries of Ethiopia, because the prophet, Zephaniah mentioned: "From beyond the rivers of Ethiopia . . . the

daughters of my dispersed." There was a period of over six
hundred years between Zephaniah and Philo; and considering the new waves of immigrants coming into Africa, they
had six hundred years to penetrate toward all the borders
of Ethiopia. E. Schurer wrote that Hebrewism was detectable
by its inscriptions from the Egyptian border westward across
North Africa to Mauretania. A. H. Godbey[38] says Jerome
(340-420 A.D., one of the four Doctors of the Church) wrote
that the Jews were spread from the western extremity of
Mauretania to India. Now, ancient Mauretania included
part of the territory on the Atlantic Ocean, Morocco, and
part of modern Algeria. It is certain that the Jews had
migrated all across North Africa by the second century.
Some scholars fix the date earlier than this.

   The Greek historian and geographer, Strabo (63 B.C.-
24 A.D.) said, concerning the Jews of Cyrene (Libya): "Now
these Jews already have gotten into all cities, and it is hard
to find a place in the habitable earth that has not admitted
this tribe of men and is not possessed by it; and it has come
to pass that Egypt and Cyrene, as having the same governors,
and a great many other nations imitate their way of living,
mantain great bodies of these Jews in a peculiar manner
(privileged status), and grow up to greater prosperity with
them and make use of the same laws with that nation also."

   After the fall of the Carthaginian metropolis in North
Africa, Roman power became dominant in the Barbery
States.[39]

   Under Roman suzerainty and power, the Jews of Asia
and North Africa rebelled A.D. 115. The Jews considered
themselves numerous enough to challenge Roman authority
in the east and the south. Because of their numbers, the
Jews almost subdued their adversaries who had compelled
them to suffer many atrocities and indignities. Emperor
Trajan sent his general, Turbo, to bring law and order.
Instead of bringing law and order, the act of supression of
the insurrection brought a massacre. The suppression of
rebellion under the slogan of "law and order" may be good

in principle; but a good thing may be carried too far; so it was in this case. The pagans and the Romans attacked the Jews indiscriminately, both the Jewish soldiers and the uninvolved peaceful population, without mercy. As a result of this merciless attack, many Jews fled to those parts of northwest Africa known as Tunisia, Algeria, Morocco, and Mauretania. Many other Jews fled to the areas where Rome did not have any jurisdiction, this was to the region of the south, the Sahara Desert and the Sudan.[40] Grayzel says: "Such is the explanation of how the Sahara Desert first acquired Jewish tribes toughened by a fighting tradition and possessed of physical characteristics [blacks] which, it is said, still make them approximate very closely the original Jewish population of Palestine."

The Jews are a omnipresent people; they seem to exist everywhere. At the beginning of the sixth century they are found in Spain before the Mohammedan conquest. Spain is known to the Jews as the classical land of crypto-Judaism, because they feigned Christianity but practiced Jewish ritual in secret. As early as the Roman period, the Jews of Spain had been large in number and influential. Many of them claimed to be descendants of noble Jews in Jerusalem who had been carried into exile by General Titus. After the Visigoth (a Germanic tribe) invasion, the situation ameliorated for the Jews because the Visigoths adopted the Arian form of Christianity and they favored the Jews. However, when they converted to Catholicism, they became zealous like any other neophytes. King Reccared ascended the throne in 589; this was the beginning of harsh religious enactments against the Jews. When King Sisebut (or Sisibot) occupied the throne, there was a prevalance of the utmost religious fanaticism. In 616 A.D. the big shock came; the king ordered the baptism of all the Jews in his domain, under the penalty of expulsion and the loss of all their property. According to Catholic authorities, ninety thousand embraced Christianity at this time. This was forced baptism. In the seventh century the Jews were threatened with the penalty of slavery if they were found practicing Judaism. This cruel policy caused many Jews to flee to the Mediterranean and western coast of Africa.[41] The southernmost point of Spain after you cross the sea leads you to the northern or the western coast of Africa. Throughout the Middle Ages many European governments expelled their Jews; these black Jews migrated to neighboring countries, Turkey and Africa.

> The Lord shall cause thee to be smitten before thine enemies: thou shalt go out one way against them, and flee seven ways before them: and shalt be removed into all the kingdoms of the earth (Deut. 28:25).

The Byzantine emperors, in the fifth and sixth centuries, persecuted the Jews constantly; therefore, multitudes of Jews were compelled to migrate into the Sahara Desert to the south.[42] By this time the Sahara Desert was heavily occupied with black Jews.

The Arabs pushed their way out of Arabia in the seventh century. In the year 640 A.D., they attacked Egypt and continued across Africa. Then a Jewish Queen named Diah Cahena organized an army consisting of Jews and Berbers in order to stop the penetration of the Moslems in north Africa. This Queen vanquished the Arabs, and the people of Africa rejoiced in her victory. Years later, the Mohammedans fought the army of this Jewish Queen once more and she was defeated. She was defeated the second time because of the jealousies of different people in various tribes. Having become disgusted, her son turned Moslem and participated in the Islamic conquest of Spain in the year 711 A.D.

THE BLACK JEWISH EMPIRE OF GHANA

The ancient black empire of Ghana was established in the western Sudan. During the colonial period, the western Sudan was called French West Africa: the northern boundary of this region is the Sahara Desert; the western and southern border is Lake Chad. Some rivers of this region are the

Senegal, the Gambia, the Volta, the Benue, the Logone, and last but not least is the famous Niger River. This river flows from the Guinea highlands northeast to the famous cities of Timbuktu and Gao; then it makes a sharp turn and flows southeast toward the city of Benin in Nigeria.

In ancient times, the Carthaginians from north Africa penetrated the Sahara Desert and the western Sudan during the second and third centuries B.C. When north and eastern Africa had amassed over a million Jews, these Jews began a continuous migration to the region of the Niger River. According to the researches of Nahum Slouschz: "The tradition of the Jewish traders in the Sahara stretches back to biblical times."[43] Slouschz continues: "And it is not at all surprising to encounter in every part of the desert traces— and even survivals—of a primitive Judaism which at one time played an important role in the whole region of the Sahara from Senegal to the very borders of Somaliland."[44] As I have mentioned earlier, this region that extends across the entire width of Africa, below the Sahara Desert from Senegal to Somaliland, is known as the Sudan or black Africa.

Between the second and the third centuries, the black Jews of Arabia continued migrating across the Red Sea to Ethiopia. The largest exodus of the Jews occurred during the persecution by the Arabs led by Mohammed. He had said on his dying bed that he wanted Islam to be supreme throughout all of Arabia.

There was a Jewish tribe called Rechab which crossed the Red Sea and migrated to the extreme point of the western Sudan.[45]

At the same time that the Jews were migrating westward across the Sudan from Ethiopia, they also migrated southward from Libya, Tunisia, Algeria, and Morocco, to the fertile region between the Senegal and Niger rivers. When the Jews from the north and the east met between these two rivers, they established a confluence or crossroad in west Africa, where men could exchange their culture, ideas, and merchandise. These Jewish migrations went on with great frequency about 300 A.D., and they continued with the utmost regularity for twelve hundred years. Joseph J. Williams[46] points out the course of the Jewish migration from northeastern Africa. He writes that the Jews migrated up the Nile passing Memphis, Elephantine,[47] Khartum, and then they turned west at Kordofan in central Sudan. In the region of the White Nile, Williams thinks some Jews settled in the country of the Shilluk, in the southern Sudan and Uganda. He continues by tracing the migration from Kordofan (going west) to Darfur, Lake Chad, Kano and then to the countries of the Niger River.

The original habitation of the Songhay people was Gounguia, Koukya, or Kuka. This place was situated in the Dendi country and known as Dendina, lying near the Niger River on the northwestern border of what is now the modern state of Nigeria. Many scholars think that the Songhay people came from Egypt or Ethiopia, because there exist many Egyptian culture complexes among them; for example, the preparation of the dead body for burial.

Za el Yemeni came to Kuka about 300 A.D.; an ancient abode of the Songhay tribe. He established a line of kings known as the Za, Dja, or the Dia Dynasty. This founder of the first Sudanic Dynasty in western Africa was a black Jew;[48] his name is sometimes written Za-al Ayaman. Joseph J. Williams says that a citizen of Timbuktu named Abderrahman Es-Sadi wrote (1652) in his book *Tarika es Sudan (History of the Sudan)* that Za-al-Ayaman was derived from dza min el-Yemen, which means, he is come from Yemen. Za el Yemeni came to the Niger country by way of Wargla in central Algeria; Wargla was a great trading center of the black Jews. Dr. Barth and Professor Godbey say that Za, the founder of the First Jewish Dynasty, established his capital later at Gao, on the eastern Upper Niger River.

The Arabs, Moors, and the Sudanic writers attribute to the ancient black African Hebrews the establishment of the first empires, "the erection of the first public buildings in the country, the construction of the first canals and irrigation systems, and the institution of a social economic regime which still survives in all Saharan communities."[49]

By what factors can we explain the emergence of black Hebrew hegemony and leadership over the indigenous tribes? The answer is simple: The Jews came into the western Sudan from northern and eastern Africa as a result of a chain of commercial and persecutory migrations. The Jews had settled among the most civilized people throughout the ages. They adopted new methods from other people and left their material, educational, and moral imprint among the people with whom they resided. For many centuries the Hebrews had to employ great physical and psychological initiative. They could not afford to be complacent or apathetic; they were hated, so apathy could mean cultural stagnation or death. The Jews imported into the western part of Africa a superior material, educational, and moral culture soon after 300 A.D., and this cultural advancement was not duplicated or exceeded until the ascendancy of the Mohammedan leader Mansa Kankan Musa of Mali in 1312 A.D. In the third and fourth centuries A.D., the Africans on the west coast did not possess the cultural superiority of the Africans on the north and east coasts.

The black Jews had an advantage over the African tribes: they carried their culture, history, laws, and written records with them; this assured them a constant precedent for the development of a higher social organization. Because of the stability of the black Jewish culture, the Jews were not absorbed into the autochthonous population. In fact, the Jews absorbed some of the native tribes. The Jews made use of every opportunity; they were an industrious and skillful people: In the Jewish Ghanaian states were found kings, princes, governors, generals, secretaries, treasurers, revenue agents, judges, architects, engineers, doctors, historians, language interpreters, mathematicians, jewelers, sculptors, masons, carpenters, painters of art, goldsmiths, leather-workers, potters, armorers, saddlers, blacksmiths, agriculturists, etcetera.

The black Hebrew kings of Ghana had two titles: (1)

Kayamaga (master of gold); (2) and Ghana (war chief).
Professor Godbey says that twenty-two Hebrew kings reigned
in Ghana before the Hegira in 622 A.D., and forty-four had
reigned by 790.[50] Davidson makes mention of the *Tarikh el
Fettach (History of the Researcher)* which says that Kumbi
had been the capital of the vast country of the Kayamaga,
while the *Tarikh es Sudan* states that Kayamaga had been
the name of the first king of this country. It is apparent that
all the kings of Ghana were called by the title Kayamaga.
And concerning Kumbi, the ancient capital of Ghana, it was
located in the southern part of the present country of Mali.
During the Middle Ages the name Ghana was not used to
designate the country; the name of this country was Aoukar,
and Ghana was just the title of its kings. Having cognizance
of this fact indicates the greatness and splendor of those
kings, because after the decline of the Za Dynasty men began
to call this country after the title of its kings, which is Ghana,
and I shall do the same.

In the fourteenth century a Muslim writer named Ibn
Batuta wrote about the women in one of the cities of Ghana.
He found the women of Walata of surpassing beauty, and
he should have known what he was talking about because
he had traveled widely. Moreover, he found another fact
astounding: The women were given more respect than the
men, and the males did not express any resentment or
jealousy. The people did not trace their descent from a pa-
ternal head but from their maternal brother. An individual
bequeathed his legacy to his sister's sons.

The material foundation of the Ghanaian state was based
on the affluence of gold and iron. The use of iron in Africa,
especially Ghana, revolutionized the social and military systems. El Zouhri stated that the Ghanaians fought many wars
against their neighbors, who did not use iron, but fought
with bars of ebony. The Ghanaians could destroy their enemies because they fought with lances and swords. The king's
revenue agents levied taxes on imports and exports and the
medium of exchange was gold.

Concerning the kingdom of Ghana, Joseph William

writes: "Whatever may be thought of the more or less mytho-
logical traditions connected with the earliest Jews in North
Africa, it is now practically an established fact that a Jewish
nation—Jewish at least in faith, and perhaps too in origin—
long held sway south of the Sahara."[51]

ELDAD THE DANITE

In the ninth century a black African Hebrew arrived in
the city of Kairouan in Algeria. In this city was one of the
famous Talmudic schools. The name of this Hebrew was
Eldad the Danite. He told a credible story of a Hebrew empire south of the Sahara in the western Sudan. According
to Eldad the Danite, the Hebrews in the interior of Africa
spoke a Phoenician-Hebraic language mixed with Arabic.
They had a religion which had come down from Moses and
a Hebrew emperor. It was believed that this emperor was
named Tloutan or Boulatan. Eldad said that the people of
this tribe had fled from the kingdom of Israel after Sennacherib, the Assyrian, had subdued it, and that other Israelite
tribes such as Naphtali, Gad, and Asher were in the land
from which he came. He told of the laws of Moses which
they followed, the complete series of the Scriptures except
Esther and Lamentations. He did not speak of the legal
works that were produced in Babylon and Palestine after
the destruction of the First Temple of which the Algerian
Jews had a knowledge. These extraordinary works were the
Mishna and the Talmud. Eldad displayed as evidence some
ceremony pertaining to the slaughtering of animals for food;
it was written in Hebrew with an Arabic tinge but Eldad
claimed that he knew no other language than Hebrew. In
regard to Eldad's story, the Gaon (head of the Jews) assured
the people that the story was credible.[52]

We are grateful for the travels and researches of Nahum
Slouschz who wrote in the early part of the twentieth century. He said: "For many years the author of this book has
been gathering material for a history of the Jewish migra-

tions into the Sahara and the Sudan. One part of his work is already done, the establishing of the authenticity of these migrations. To the writing of the Arabs and the oral traditions of the country he can now add the archeological evidence furnished by the ruins of ancient Jewish cities in the Sahara and the Sudan, and the documentary evidence of Hebrew inscriptions, like those of Tuat, which date from the thirteenth and fourteenth centuries."[53]

It is now an established fact that Ghana was a black Hebrew state and at this juncture I shall continue my writings concerning the Za Dynasty of Ghana.

The fifteenth Za prince[54] took control of the great city of Gao on the Upper Niger, A.D. 1009. His name was Za Kasi or Kossoi. Up to this time all the kings of Ghana professed the Hebrew religion; however, in this year a radical transformation occurred: Za Kasi accepted Islam. Davidson, quoting the *Tarikh el Fettach*, says that the King of Songhay (Ghana) was persuaded to convert to Islam by the merchants of the city of Gao, who already had become wealthy and economically powerful. Much of Ghana's trade was maintained with the Muslims of the north. The north Africans were ardent Mohammedans in their day; and economics and religion were co-partners, operating concertedly in the city of Gao. I do not condemn Za Kasi for his conversion to Islam; in fact I shall justify his actions. The Muslims were dominating Ghana's vital trade links in North Africa and the Sahara and it was good for Ghana's security to be recognized as having a Mohammedan king.

Concerning Islam in the western Sudan, Basil Davidson[55] makes the following observation: "Islam reaches the markets of the western Sudan by at least the ninth century. But it makes little initial impact. The rulers of Ghana do not accept Islam as one of their state religions. Only at the beginning of the eleventh century are there a few such conversions, the earliest of any importance of which we know being that of the king of Gao, traditionally in 1010, followed by that of the king of Kanem-Bornu in 1086." Davidson says: "These are tactical conversions (these kings are Moslems only in name), motivated as much by commercial convenience as by appreciation of the political and religious achievements and teaching of Islam."

In spite of the fact that the kings of Ghana professed Islam, many of the inhabitants remained Jews. El Bekri, the Moslem writer, wrote about Ghana in 1067. The King of Ghana, in his day, was Tenkamenin, who came to the throne A.D. 1062. El Bekri says that the King of Ghana, Tenkamenin, was the ruler of a great empire and he was able to organize an army of two hundred thousand men.[56]

In the eleventh century a Mohammedan people from the northwest invaded the city of Aoudaghast within the Empire of Ghana. These invaders were called the Almoravides. By the year 1076 A.D. Abu Bakr, the leader of the Almoravides, captured the capital of Ghana; however, the Islamic-Jewish king was allowed to maintain his throne; Tenkamenin paid tribute to Abu Bakr.

At this time Gao or Gagho, the capital of Ghana, was separated into two cities; the first one was the residence of the king. This city contained a fortress which was surrounded by a wall. The second city contained twelve mosques in which the Mohammedan merchants could settle or wait until they transacted their business. This description given by El Bekri leaves us with the impression that the city of the king's residence was probably inhabited mainly by Jews, because there was a great distinction between the king's residence and the residence of the Mohammedans.

In the city of Gao the Islamic religion was influential, only a Moslem could be king.[57] When a new king ascended the throne, three royal imperial emblems constituting the Koran, a sword, and a ring were received by the king.

Ahmed Baba, a native of Songhay, dates the beginning of Islam in Ghana after the year 1010. El Bekri designates the then reigning king as Kanda. Barth says that he is most probably identical with the Islamic-Jewish king Za Bayuki or Bayarkoy Kaima (of Ahmed Baba) the third succeeding king of Za Kasi.[58]

THE EMPIRE OF MALI

The empire of Mali is also called the Mellestine empire. The word Mali is derived from a Mandingo grammatical root meaning free. The rulers and people of the empire of Mali were black Africans of the Mandingo tribe. This tribe was originally situated in the territory known today as Guinea Sierra Leone and northward. On the banks of the Upper Niger near the present-day Sierra Leone, the Mandingos established their capital at a place called Niani.

After the break-up of the Ghanaian Empire by invasions from many tribes, Ghana split apart into a number of states. But in the capital of Ghana, Gao, the Hebrew Za kings continued to reign.

Many people who were subject to Ghana proclaimed their independence after chaos set in. The most celebrated of these people were the Mandingos who established the nucleus of a new empire about the middle of the thirteenth century (1240 A.D.).

There are several important factors that we must consider in order to comprehend the rise of Mali. First of all, Mali had received an impetus and significant influence from her predecessor Ghana to the north. This influence can be explained in political, economic, and religious ways. The Muslim merchants of the north and the Sahara had their trading centers in the cities of Ghana. The Mandingo traders of Mali traded with the Muslims. In those days, and to some extent today, commerce and religion have operated together. The Mandingo merchants recognized the advantages of the rapidly growing powerful influential culture and religion of the Muslims in the north. As a result, the Mandingo merchants played a great part in the transportation of Islam to their people.

The Mandingos were a successful agricultural people. They were blessed with the availability of rivers which they used for irrigation. They grew rice and other staples which contributed to a rapidly growing population. The people of Mali had enough grain to sell to the people of the Sahara and the north. They developed market-towns which later grew into cities and states. With their trading abilities, their skills and vigorous energy, Davidson said, the Mandingos became "rich." Davidson continued: "With the collapse of Ghana (as an empire), their chance of large political power was open. They grasped it with a sure hand."

In dealing with the kings of Mali, Ibn Khaldun is rated as our best authority. He wrote about 1376 A.D.

The King of Mali who is rendered credit for the establishment and organization of an imperial system in Mali was Sundiata. The year that the Mandingo state rose to imperial power is dated from 1240. In this year a decisive battle was fought between the Mandingos and a people from Tekrur, evidently Almoravides from medieval Mauretania. Sundiata defeated Sumanguru and his people, who had captured the seat of the Hebrew kings of Ghana and imposed a tribute on them. Like other kings of the western Sudan, Sundiata knew that power was contingent on wealth; most of the wealth was in trade; and most of the trade was in the hands of Muslims; consequently he converted to Islam.

Almost a hundred years after the death of Sundiata, a powerful king emerged in Mali. His name was Mansa Musa. During his lifetime (1312-1337), his accomplishments transcended his predecessors'. His empire extended from east to west, beginning at the Atlantic Ocean to northern modern Nigeria; and from north to south, reaching almost from central Mauretania and extending to the borders of modern Guinea and the Ivory Coast.

In 1326 A.D. Mansa Musa made a pilgrimage to Mecca, the Holy City of the Mohammedans. It is said that he exhibited a marvelous splendor that astonished the spectators: He arrived in the east with thousands of foot soldiers, and over 60,000 mounted warriors. In addition to his soldiers he had five hundred slaves, each carrying a rod of gold weighing six pounds. As a contribution to the holy cities, he gave 20,000 pieces of gold.

Mali, in its heyday was known for its prosperity and peace; within the empire existed one pervading system of law, order, and justice. An African visitor, Ibn Batuta, had this to say about the Sudan: "The inhabitants had a greater abhorrence of injustice than any other people. Neither the man who travels nor he who stays at home has anything to fear from robbers or men of violence." This fact might seem incredible to those people who think that black men are innately violent.

During the lifetime of Mansa Musa, commerce increased on a large scale. The merchants of Mali established relay stations throughout the empire at important centers; these enterprises reached the forest country south of the Senegal and the Niger rivers.

Before the time of Mansa Musa, the city of Timbuktu was founded in the latter part of the eleventh century. Barth thinks that it was first a small marketplace for the inhabitants of the province of Rad.

Mansa Musa is not only remembered for his pilgrimage, trade and military accomplishments, but also for his public constructions. The king of Mali built a palace and several mosques in the celebrated city of Timbuktu. At the extremities of the city of Timbuktu, these mosques were erected: The mosque of Jengere-ber was located in the southwest and the mosque of Sankore was located in the northern quarter of the city. Mansa Musa was, indeed, a champion of Islamic religion and learning. This was the time that the city of Timbuktu and Jenne began to rise as scholastic cities. Concomitant with the mosque of Sankore was established also the University of Sankore.[59] This university during the period of the dynasty of Askia the Great acquired a universal reputation as a university of theology, law, philosophy, medicine, history, etcetera.

Before I shall continue, it behooves me to explain to you that the later empire of Songhay was erected on the foundation of the empire of Ghana. The only difference was that Songhay was greater in land area, more Islamic, more scholastic and it terminated with a native African king.

When the emperor Kankan Musa was on his pilgrimage in Arabia, Sagamandir, the general of Mali, took Gao the capital of Ghana or Songhay. Then Kankan Musa returned from Arabia by way of Gao and accepted the capitulation of the king of Ghana and its nobles. Philip St. Laurent, who writes a monthly article on African history (see *Tuesday Magazine*) for the Philadelphia *Bulletin* says that the soldiers of Mali were made prisoners of the ruling family of Dia Soboi (this was the Za Hebrew Dynasty). Among these prisoners were Ali Kolon, or Killun, and his brother Selmar Nar, the sons of Za Yasebi; these Hebrew princes were appointed as pages at the court of Mali about 1335 A.D.[60] In the meantime, Gao was subjected under the Mali political system says Davidson, and the Mansa Kankan Musa exacted tribute from its rulers.

It was not too long before the princes of the Za Dynasty escaped from the court and army of Mali. They organized an army and fought the king of Mali. Ali Kolon entertained a profound hatred against the Mali conquerors because they had subjugated his people. In the latter part of the fourteenth century, the army of Ali Kolon (later called Sonni, the liberator, Ali) made attacks on Niani the capital of Mali. Yearning for independence, Sonni Ali desisted in paying tribute to Mali. Because of the exploits of Sonni Ali, the Za Dynasty of Gao acquired a new appellation; the dynasty after Sonni Ali I is called the Sonni or Shi Dynasty. There were about seventeen or eighteen Islamic-Hebrew kings in this dynasty.

THE EMPIRE OF SONGHAY

In the year 1464, the sixteenth[61] Za prince Sonni Ali took the leadership of Gao and began to build a new empire. Sonni Ali attacked many of the neighboring tribes, including the city of Timbuktu, and brought them under his hegemony. For his strength, he did not depend too much on the Muslims of the cities but primarily on the inhabitants of the countryside. Sonni Ali was not even a good Muslim; he adhered to the traditional religion of Gao and the Songhay people. In almost every way, Songhay was a greater empire than Mali. Sonni Ali systematized various schemes of organization and administration unknown by his predecessors. He appointed governors over his territories and organized a standing professional army consisting of an echelon, including a navy, on the Niger.

The Songhay empire seems to have begun with Sonni Ali I. This was the time of the decline of the empire of Mali in the year 1350 A.D., but the superior vigor of the Songhay empire did not occur until the time of Askia the Great.

Now, pertaining to the temperament of Sonni Ali, many writers say that it was uncontrollable. He would put to death many of his important officials and ministers of state, later wishing they were alive. Sonni Ali's secretary at this time was a man named El Cadr for whom Sonni Ali had ordered the death penalty because of a contradiction. In the course of time a book arrived that no one in the king's court could read but El Cadr; then the king expressed remorse for his rash action; at that juncture his secretary was brought into his presence. On seeing him, Sonni Ali displayed great joy and gave valuable gifts to those who saved him.

There was another distinguished officer of the state, who survived death in this manner, known by various names such as Mohammed Toure and Abu Bekr who succeeded Sonni Ali as Askia the Great.

After Sonni Ali had completed his business in Gao, his unconquerable military impulse moved him on. He attacked to the east and the west expanding the empire. His predatory acts acquired for him much booty, but a change of fortune caused his death. When he was crossing the Koni River, he fell into the torrent and was drowned. The body of the great king was prepared and preserved according to the ancient Egyptian custom; this custom consisted of the extraction of the intestines and the insertion of honey.

Sonni Barro, sometimes called Abu Kebr, succeeded Sonni Ali on the throne but his reign was very short. After the death of Sonni Ali, his most distinguished general, Mohammed Toure plunged the empire into civil war. Mohammed Toure fought Sonni Barro at Dangha and defeated him, then Barro took refuge at Gao, the capital. Mohammed Toure stopped for a while in order to reorganize his army before resuming the war. After a prolonged and bloody battle Sonni Barro was conquered and forced into exile. When hearing that Mohammed had seized the kingdom from Barro, the daughters of Sonni Ali were said to have exclaimed, "Askia! Askia! Usurper!"

As a result of this, Mohammed immediately decreed that he be called by no other name than Askia and he became known as Mohammed Askia, the founder of a native African dynasty, the last to exist in this part of the Sudan. With the rise of the Askian Dynasty the Za-Sonni Dynasty of the black Hebrew kings was terminated about the year 1492 A.D.[62]

To perpetuate his illegal rule, Mohammed Askia employed political cunning; he became a zealous Moslem and secured the confirmation of the ecclesiastical authorities. He advocated that Mohammedanism should be spread throughout the empire. Askia discharged a group of soothsayers and surrounded himself with theologians. He consulted with them on many important matters. With Askia's urging, the theologians proclaimed a declaration which said: Sonni Ali was a heretic and that the struggle against Sonni Barro was a holy war.

About three years after the civil war Askia emulated Mansa Kankan Musa of Mali by undertaking a long pilgrimage to the holy cities in the east. His cavalcade consisted of a vast number of infantrymen and cavaliers. On this pilgrimage was also a retinue of 1500 princes and chiefs of the empire. While Askia was in Mecca, he spent 100,000 pieces of gold; this was more than any other ruler had spent. In Mecca he purchased a garden and set up a charitable institution for the people of the Sudan. He gave to the Khalif of Bagdad gifts that astonished the entire court; these contributions surpassed all other kings. The Khalif of Bagdad, Abassid Motewekkel, was immensely impressed with Askia. With the Khalif's consent, Askia was made his deputy in Songhay and as a sign of his authority, the Khalif gave Askia a green fez and a white turban.

In Cairo, Egypt, Askia passed many hours among the religious scholars, forming a special acquaintance with a scholar named Essoyouti. It was here in Cairo that Askia accepted many advanced concepts about political science which he put into practice in the Sudan.

Askia returned to his homeland with an enlarged mind and many new experiences. He appointed his brother, Omar, commander of the army, and he began to consolidate the expanding empire initiated by Sonni Ali.

Attacking many tribes (unbelievers in Islam), Askia declared war on the Yollofs and the Mossi. At first, he sent an ambassador to the king of the Mossi, demanding that the king convert to Islam. The king refused and Askia displayed no mercy in the war that followed. He decimated the Mossi hamlets and towns, making all the inhabitants prisoners and forced them all to become Muslims. The length of his empire extended from the Atlantic Ocean beyond Lake Chad in the east.

After the year 1502 the army of Askia invaded the state of Mali. The Songhays sustained such a large number of fatalities that Omar remarked, "The Songhay will be exterminated." The reply of Askia was: "On the contrary. The conquered nations will make our lives easier, for they will be part of us and will assist us in our enterprises."

But Askia is known for more than his conquests. Writes Davidson: "The literate culture of the Western Sudan, already in existence for several hundred years, flowered in Timbuktu during years that saw, in Europe, the ravage of

the Hundred Year War. No one can say how much it flowered, nor what fruits it bore, for the books that men read
or wrote there are lost or not yet found; but Leo Africanus,
two centuries later, gives some measure of the city's intellectual life. 'In Timbuktu,' he says, 'there are numerous
judges, doctors and clerics, all receiving good salaries from
the king. He pays great respect to men of learning. There is
a big demand for books in manuscripts imported from Barbary. More profit is made from the book trade than from
any other line of business! The king, of course, was Askia
the Great.' "

Whereas Gao was the political capital of the Songhay
Empire, Timbuktu was the cultural capital. Many of the
students of Timbuktu, Gao, and Jenne, were sent to the
Moslem universities of North Africa, Spain, and Asia. Also,
many learned men, irrespective of nationality, were sum-
moned to stay at the celebrated city of Timbuktu, where
money was appropriated for their learning.

In order to unite his empire, Askia interlocked the royal
families by marriage. Says Du Bois: "The highest officers
of state were either chosen from the royal family or married to its princesses, as were the principal military chiefs,
forming a dynastic aristocracy of the greatest importance to
national unity."

For better administrative organization, Askia set up four
viceroys in his empire; one in the east around Lake Chad,
a second one was in the north around Timbuktu and Gao,
a third one was in the northwest, and a fourth in the southwest. Because the government of Songhay was strong, Askia
was able to control the commerce. He built a merchant fleet
and war fleet to facilitate commerce in the harbors and
canals that he constructed on the Niger River and its
branches. As a result, the economy and commerce developed
with a tremendous upsurge. The city of Jenne became a
melting pot of internal commerce; Timbuktu of international commerce.

For the first time, the Portuguese established trading

companies on the west coast of Africa in the year 1448. During the lifetime of Askia, north African and Portuguese ships sailed to the Songhay port at Kabara, in the center of the Niger. In order to perpetuate and facilitate trade, Askia standardized the system of weights and measures. There was no toleration of highway robbery. Anybody found culpable of this overt act incurred the utmost punishment.

During the reign of Askia I, his son, Askia Moussa, revolted and expelled his father. Years later, with the help of another son (Ismail) he returned to Gao, the capital. After reigning for thirty-five years, he died in 1538.

Despite the fact that there existed much debauchery among Askia's descendants, the strong government he created insured its survival for many years.

Final chaos came to Songhay when the Moors invaded in 1591. The Moors came to acquire wealth; they paid a dire price for their predatory exploits. Some writers have estimated that 23,000 Moors perished in one way or another in the military campaigns against Songhay. After two decades, the Moors withdrew their military forces from Songhay, in 1618. Basil Davidson has this to say about Songhay: "But if their invasion cost the Moroccans much more than it was worth, it cost Songhay its place in history. For it demolished the unity and the administrative organization of the state, and while it left Timbuktu and Gao and Djenne as considerable cities, it robbed this civilization of its vitality. . . . 'From that moment,' says the chronicle (the *Tarikh*), 'everything changed. Danger took the place of security, poverty of wealth. Peace gave way to distress, disasters, and violence.' "

After the Moors withdrew from the Sudan, the Portuguese, French, and English established colonies and seized the mineral resources of these countries.

CHAPTER VI

The Final Dispersion of the Black Jews of Africa

EARLY NORTH AFRICA

Many scholars call the inhabitants of North Africa "Berbers," but I shall not do so. I do not like this word Berber; first of all, it is not a native word of Africa, therefore it is misleading. The Greeks and Romans called the people of North Africa "Berbers" which means barbarians; however, the people of this region have their own names. The unbiased Greek historian, Herodotus (may honor be given unto him), gives the original names of the tribes of North Africa. Beginning from Egypt extending to the Atlantic Ocean they are as follows: Adyrmachidae, Gilligammae, Asbytae, Auschisae, Cabalians, Nasamonians, Numidians, Psylli, Garamantians, Macae, Gindanes, Lolophagi, Machlyans, Auseans, Troglodytes, Zavecians, Gyzantians, Atarantians, and the Atlantes.[1]

Herodotus says there are four nations in Africa; two are indigenous, Ethiopians and Libyans. The Phoenicians and Greeks are newcomers. Herodotus considered all the north African tribes to be Libyans and all the Africans below the Sahara he called Ethiopians. These are his two indigenous nations in Africa.[2]

The original inhabitants of North Africa were Hamites;

these Hamites were black like the Egyptians and this point has been proven by Herodotus.[3]

Because most of the history in the western World has been distorted, it becomes necessary for me to explain to you some of these distortions. Says Heinrich Barth, a European writer: "The inhabitants of Walata[4] are a mixed race of blacks and whites." Now, the question is, "whom does he include as his whites? Continues Barth: "The whites are Berbers and Arabs."[5] These Berbers and Arabs were not whites in ancient times. What is his basis for calling them whites? The obvious reason is that he wants to attribute ancient advanced civilization to the white race in order to perpetuate the philosophy of white supremacy. Many black people have straight noses and thin lips; the black people that possess these qualities are said to have a white morphology (form). Joseph Williams has this to say about the blacks of West Africa: "In most mixed group of Negroes a Songhois may be identified at first glance; his skin is black as theirs, certainly, but nothing in his mask conforms to their well known characteristics. The nose of the Songhois is straight and long, pointed rather than flat; the lips are comparatively thin; and the mouth wide rather than prominent and broad, while the eyes are deeply set and straight in their orbits. A cursory glance shows that the profile resembles that of the European."[6] Some European writers even penetrate into the blackest Africa and divide the blacks according to the shape of their noses and lips. Continues Williams: The Songhays, "though black-skinned and woolly-haired, their features are often of Caucasian cast."[7] There are many colored people in the United States with straight noses and thin lips, even as black as tar; and the Europeans do not classify these colored people as belonging to the white race. After extensive research, my conclusion is this: Some European writers have classified certain tribes in Africa and Asia as belonging to the white race; they do this as long as it is psychologically advantageous, in order to inflate their ego, and to give them a prominent place in Afro-Asian history.

Not only were the people of Africa and Asia black in ancient times, but also the European lands of the Mediterranean.[8]

THE CANAANITES AND PHOENICIANS IN AFRICA

The language which is called Hebrew-Phoenician or Canaanite was employed in the lands called Phoenicia, Palestine, or Canaan for over a thousand years before the Aramaeans, Abraham, Isaac, and Jacob, came to Canaan. The Israelites lost their Aramaic language and adopted the Hebrew speech of the Canaanites. The Hebrew-Phoenician merchants from the cities of Sidon and Tyre controlled the trade along the Mediterranean coasts for more than a thousand years before there were any economic treaties made with the Israelites. The Hebrew-speaking Phoenicians (Canaanites) established their greatest city, Carthage at Tunis in North Africa; all the Canaanites were black people.

Before the Phoenicians established their colony (Carthage) in Africa, many Hebrew-speaking Canaanites had migrated across northern Africa.

One Tosefta,[9] quoting an older source, says that when Joshua approached Canaan, he told the inhabitants that three courses were open to them: they could either leave the country, or they could sue for peace, or they could declare war against him. The Girgashites, among others, preferred to withdraw into Africa. The Tosefta goes on to say that the Amorites, the Kadmoni, the Kenites and the Kenezites—some of whom figure among the founders of Carthage —also went to Africa. These traditions date from a period when communication between Africa and Phoenicia was continuous. The proper names of Girgash and Kenaz are often met with in Carthaginian and Phoenician inscriptions.

The Talmud[10] says that the Canaanites in Africa asked Alexander the Great to restore to them their country, which had been taken from their ancestors by Joshua ben Nun.

"These traditions . . . have been ratified by the Fathers of the Church; thus St. Jerome calls to witness the Talmud to support his statement that the Girgashites established colonies in Africa;[11] and Saint Augustine designates the natives of Africa as 'Canaanites.' "[12]

The prophet Isaiah (19:18) says that five cities in Africa will speak the language of Canaan.

We should not forget that the Israelites have been engaged in commercial enterprises, activities, and migrations since Solomon's treaty with the Phoenicians.

The Phoenicians established their metropolis, Carthage, in the ninth century B.C. Eventually they conquered the neighboring tribes from Libya to the Atlantic Ocean, disseminating their Hebrew-Phoenician language and culture in every direction. The Hebrew-Phoenician language and culture were invigorated and strengthened by the deportation and the migration of energetic black Hebrews from Palestine. Ptolemy Soter[13] of Egypt conquered Syria and Phoenicia, deporting more than 100,000 Hebrews. The Persian king (Cambyses) had previously sanctioned the colonization of Hebrews in Egypt. During the wars of the Maccabees, thousands of Hebrews became slaves and exiles. Ptolemy Lathyrus captured 10,000 slaves from the region of the Sea of Galilee. The kings of Egypt, Psamtik I and Psamtik II, used Israelite garrisons on the Egyptian borders near Libya. The wars with Rome compelled hundreds of thousands more to escape into North Africa.

During the Punic Wars and after, North Africa contained a large Hebrew population; this Hebrew population made converts and intermarried with the Canaanites and the native Africans.

THE CITY AND LANGUAGE OF HANNIBAL

At the ruins of Carthage, archeologists have found about four thousand inscriptions in the ancient language of Canaan. Nahum Slouschz says these inscriptions date from

the time of Nehemiah, of Simon the Just, of Hannibal and
of Hasdrubal. Says Slouschz: "And most valuable of all, we
have found again the ancient language and writing of
Canaan, the rich, idiomatic speech of a city which once
counted seven hundred thousand inhabitants. And we Hebrew writers, we who write and feel in our biblical tongue,
have recognized at once that this re-called Phoenician language is nothing more nor less than Hebrew—a pure Hebrew
dialect, nearly the same as was spoken in the country of
Israel. . . ."

The population of Carthage was derived from Palestine
and its civilization was Hebraic in origin. Slouschz is certain,
after much research, that the language Hannibal spoke and
in which he directed his troops was Hebrew.[14]

There is evidence that the Carthaginians possessed a
high priesthood and their ceremonies and sacrifices were
similar to the rituals found in the book of Leviticus. According to some inscriptions, the Hebrew tribes of Asher
and Zebulun were in Carthage from the foundation of the
city. At the ruins of Carthage were excavated many inscriptions containing many Hebrew names such as Joab, Joas,
and Joel.

The city of Tunis is said to be neither Arab nor European. Tunis is a Jewish city. Nowhere else does the Jew
feel at home as he does in Tunis. Slouschz says so beauti-
fully: "And, indeed, Tunis, the inheritor of Hebrew Carthage, is the Eternal City of the Jews. For, like the Phoenix,
the Jews have risen again and again out of the ashes of their
destruction. After the sacking of Carthage, the Jews were
found again in Carthage under Roman domination; after
the Byzantine persecutions, they fled into the desert. . . .
And even under the persecution of the Arabs, the Jews
somehow managed to survive catastrophe after catastrophe."

THE MOORISH EMPIRE

In less than a hundred years, the black Arabs had pushed their way completely across North Africa in the seventh century. At this time the Arabs were black; they had not mixed much with other people. The Arabs did penetrate into the interior of the Sahara Desert, but only in small numbers so that the territory remained basically African.

Mulay Idris, the descendant of Ali, the son-in-law of Mohammed, brought northern Morocco under his control late in the seventh century. His son and successor was Idris II, who founded the kingdom of Fez.

At this time, in the land of Spain, the black Jews were persecuted and many had fled to Morocco for refuge. As a result of this persecution, the Jews of Morocco and the Moors planned to invade Spain with the assistance of Spanish Jews. In the meantime, the plot was uncovered and the Jews of Spain suffered for their intentions. Early in the eighth century, the Mohammedans from Morocco, united with the black Jews, made what we call an amphibious landing at Gibraltar. This invasion was successful. Nahun Slouschz says that: "The first one to set foot on the soil of Spain was General Tarif (a Jew of the tribe of Simeon),[15] after whom the island of Tarifa, opposite Tangiers, was named." However, the Rock of Gibraltar, previously known as the Pillars of Hercules, received its new name from the great Moorish conqueror Gebel al Tarik, which means the mountain of Tarik.[16]

Here is a vivid account of the conquering Moors described by a writer who sympathized with Christian Spain: ". . . the reins of their horses were as fire, their faces black as pitch, their eyes shone like burning candles, their horses were swift as leopards and the riders fiercer than a wolf in the sheepfold at night; . . . the noble Goths were broken in an hour, quicker than tongue can tell. Oh, luckless Spain!"[17]

These black Moors ruled over parts of Spain for more than seven hundred years. During this time the Moors developed the greatest cultural civilization known anywhere in Europe.

In the last half of the eleventh century, there emerged a powerful dynasty of sultans from Senegal, West Africa, known as the Almoravides. They established their capital at Marrakesh, Morocco, and became masters of a new empire that included Senegal, Morocco, Algeria, Tunis, and southern Spain; this empire was even larger than western Europe.

At this time the first general of the Senegalese was Abu Bekr, who was supplanted by a stronger general, Yusuf ben Tachfin.

Yusuf's first aim was to construct an elegant capital, with marvelous houses, a marble-floored palace, and beautiful flower-beds. The city that he built, Marrakesh or Morocco City, became the name of this country.

When Moorish power was declining in Spain, Yusuf crossed the Mediterranean into Spain in order to reinforce Moorish control. He brought 15,000 black troops with him, and defeated Alphonso VI with his 70,000 Christians at the Battle of Zalacca. During the wars of the Almoravides, the greatest commander and hero of Spanish literature was slain; his name was Roderigo Diaz de Bivar, better known as El Cid.

The Moors were known for more than just conquest. While the remaining part of Europe was in a state of ignorance, the Spanish people took advantage of the knowledge of the black Moors. During the Moorish rule, many other capitals of Europe were mere hamlets, but Cordova, the capital of Spain was a booming city. It is said that after dark one could walk many miles in Cordova and never pass through a street not lighted by public lights. When a person walked out after dark in London, he had to carry a candle or lantern with him to illuminate his path and had to wear high shoes to walk through the thick mud that often covered the roads.

When many Europeans were garbed in skins and in coarse garments, the Moors were wearing silks, linens, and cotton cloth. They also washed in nine hundred bath houses of Cordova.

The palace of the Moorish sultan or caliph was far greater in beauty, comfort and wealth than any of the castles of the medieval kings. The Moors used extremely highly polished marble in their construction. The sides of the walls were patiently carved, and the floors were made with various decorations called mosaics. It is said that the Moors were masters in mosaic work.

The Arabs and Moore were known not only for their handicraft, but also for their science. Most of the knowledge of ancient Greece and the Near East was unknown in Europe during the medieval period. The Arabs had come into close relationship with Greek and Persian culture. The Arabs did not destroy this culture; instead, they brought it to North Africa. There were many famous Moorish and Hebrew scholars in southern Spain. The black Jews, like the Arabs and Moors, made a great contribution not only to Afro-Asian civilization, but also to the European. The Jews in the East knew Greek and Syriac. They helped translate the works of the Greek philosophers into Arabic. In turn, these works were studied by the Arab-speaking Jews of North Africa and Spain and translated into the Hebrew. The black Jews of the Moorish kingdom of Spain translated these works into the Latin language, and from Spain the sciences of the Greeks and the Afro-Asian people were transmitted to western Europe.

Erudite Moorish men made spectacular contributions to philosophy, medicine, mathematics, chemistry, astronomy, and botany.

The Muslim doctors were no sawbones, but masters of their science.

They established acadamies and universities for the rich; also, there were many free schools. There were excellent libraries. The scholarly caliph of Cordova, in the tenth century, sent all over the world for books. The library of this caliph contained over four hundred thousand volumes.

Moorish normal life was based on agriculture, manufacturing, and trade. The Moors brought into Spain rice, cotton, peaches, oranges, and lemons. Silk culture was introduced into Spain by the Moors. The Moors had fine pottery, glazed tiles, silks, velvet, brocades, jewels, and ornamental leather products. Moorish civilization had a gigantic effect on Portugal and Spain; this is the reason that these two countries were the first European powers to emerge after the Dark Ages.

In the process of time the Moors were driven southward. In the eleventh century, El Cid conquered the great Moorish city of Valencia. Much later, in the thirteenth century, the king of Castile conquered Sevilla and Cordova. Afterward the Moors were pushed into a small region called Granada.

OUTSTANDING BLACK JEWS

Some of the outstanding black Jews of Portugal, Spain and North Africa were the following:

Hasdai ibn Shaprut, who lived between 925-975. He began his career as a physician and continued his interest in the medical profession, especially in drugs. Eventually, he became physician to the Khalif. Later he rendered official advice concerning diplomatic matters. He remained in the center of Hebrew scholars whom he supported. He entertained Moses ben Hanoch, a representative of the Babylonian academies, who began the foundation of Talmudic learning in Spain.

Saadia Gaon was born in 892 in the district of Fayyum, Upper Egypt. He was learned in the Bible and the Talmud, in Arabic as in Hebrew literature, in Greek and Arab philosophy. He was one of the first Hebrew grammarians and philosophic commentators of the Bible. Saadia composed special works on many subjects such as philosophy, astronomy, geography, theology, mathematics, music, poetry, chronology, and philology.

Isaac of Fez, Morocco, or Alfasi, so named because he came from the city of Fez, lived during the eleventh century. Although the first important academy was founded by Moses ben Hanoch in Cordova, the real foundation of Spanish talmudic tradition was laid by Alfasi. The interest of Alfasi was in Talmudic law, especially such as were vital for the Hebrews of the dispersion.

Samuel ibn Naghdela lived from 993-1056. He started out as a grocer. His acquisition of knowledge in the languages, mathematics, and philosophy was extraordinary. Because Samuel had a beautiful handwriting, he was appointed secretary of the grand vizier; in this position he was able to put to good use his wisdom and knowledge. When the vizier died, Samuel succeeded him as adviser to the Moorish king of Granada. On several occasions, he was appointed as the head of the Moorish armies of Granada.

Samuel ibn Naghdela was respected also in Jewish circles. The king of Granada elevated him to the position of Nagid; that is, prince or leader of the Jews.

Moses Maimonides was the outstanding black Jew during the Middle Ages; he is known as Rambam (Rabbenu Moshe ben Maimon). Moses was born in Cordova on March 30, 1135, the eve of the Passover. His father, Maimon, was an offspring of a great family of scholars and religious leaders. His family tree has been traced to Rabbi Judah the Prince, the composer of the Mishmah, to the royal house of David.

While the Talmud and Rabbinics were the chief subjects of Maimonides, he dedicated time to the sciences that were taught and postulated by the ancient Greeks and medieval Arabs. He received his learning under Hebrew and Moorish teachers, and before long he was learned in the natural sciences, mathematics, medicine, metaphysics, philosophy, and logic.

In the year 1145, when Moses was ten years of age, Abdullah-ibn-Tumart, a religious fanatic, founded the Dynasty of the Almohades.

The Almohades, who proclaimed a religion of absolute Monotheism, succeeded, after many battles, in expelling the Almoravides (black Moors from the highland of Morocco) and established their own rule over the Moorish empire.

The Almohades directed a reign of terror and persecution not only against Judaism and Christianity, but also against sectarianism in Islam. The Almohades displayed their intolerance for other religions. There were prohibitions against the existence of churches and synagogues. Jews and Christians were given the one alternative, Islam or death.

Abdulmumen, who succeeded Abdullah-ibn-Tumart, permitted heretics to depart from his country. The Christian exiles found asylum in northern Spain. It was difficult for the Jews to find a place of security, and many of them died by the sword as martyrs for their religion. Some of the Jews converted to Islam as a disguise, and remained loyal to their own faith, practicing Judaism in secret.

About the middle of the twelfth century, when Maimonides was thirteen years of age, the Almohades crossed the Mediterranean into Spain and established their power in Andalusia. In the late spring of that year, the Almohades invaded the city of Cordova, and instituted a reign of terror and persecution. The magnificent synagogues were destroyed, the Talmudic schools at Seville and Lucena were closed, and non-believers in Islam (Jews and Christians) were given the alternatives of Islam, expulsion, or death.

Because of all this turmoil and social unrest, the family of Moses Maimonides decided to depart from that inhospitable land and to sail across the Mediterranean to Morocco in northern Africa. They remained in the city of Fez for about five years and then traveled to Palestine. Because the environment was not conducive to learning, Moses moved to Egypt.

Moses Maimonides continued his studies in medicine; his fame as a physician now spread throughout Egypt and beyond. It is said that Moses was offered a position as a physician to King Richard the Lion-Hearted (leader of the Third Crusade). When Moses was about fifty years of age, he was appointed by Alfadhel, the Vizier of Egypt, as his own medical adviser, and he was given a place among the royal physicians.

Moses was also a great leader and judge of the Egyptian Jewish community. His son followed in his footsteps (religiously and secularly) receiving the leadership of the Jewish communities and as physician to the Sultan.

Other outstanding black Jews of Spain were poets such as: Solomon ibn Gabirol, Moses ibn Ezra, and Judah ha-Levi.

THE EXPULSION OF THE JEWS FROM
SPAIN AND PORTUGAL

It was A.D. 1492 (January 2nd), when the Moorish stronghold of Granada surrendered to the armies of King Ferdinand and Queen Isabella. For the first time since the year 711, all of Spain was in Christian hands. The decree to expel the Jews from Spain was signed on March 31, in one of the corridors of the great Alhambra, the palace of the Moorish kings of Granada. The reason given for the expulsion of the Jews was that it was thought they corrupted the Marranos (Jews converted to Christianity) by privately encouraging them in disloyalty to Christianity. The ultimatum given to the Jews expired August 1, 1492. But the last group of Jews did not leave until August 2, 1492. This date is of strange coincidence. That day was the 9th of Ab, the fast day which is reminiscent of the destruction of the First and Second Temples. Professor Allen H. Godbey says that the reign of the last Jewish king of Ghana terminated in 1492.

In order to satisfy Queen Isabella of Spain, King Manoel of Portugal promulgated a royal decree expelling the Jews and Moors from his country in 1496. The Jews who were expelled from Spain and Portugal were scattered throughout the Mediterranean coasts. It is estimated that over 100,000 Jews departed from Spain and Portugal during the persecutions and the expulsion. Some of these Jews went to northern Europe, Italy, and Turkey; but most of them went to Moslem countries of northern and western Africa.[18] These black Jews would naturally go to African countries most of all, because of less persecution and they could disguise themselves easily among blacks.

R. H. M. Elwes[19] gives a graphic description of the Portuguese Jew, Baruch Spinoza: "Middle-sized, good features, skin somewhat black, black curly hair, long eyebrows of the same color, so that one might know by his looks that he was a descendant from Portuguese Jews."

When the Jews were expelled from Spain, about 100,000 entered Portugal. They were permitted to enter under the condition that they pay the poll tax, with the understanding that they would leave the country within eight months. Also at this time the king obligated himself to take the Jews wherever they desired at the termination of the eight months. When the time expired, many Jews were stranded because the king did not provide enough ships in time. All the black Jews who were left behind were deprived of their freedom and sold into slavery.

During the reign of King Joao II (or John II), seven hundred black Hebrew children were ruthlessly taken away from their parents in Portugal and transported to the island of San Thome, off the west coast of Africa.[20] This island is located near Nigeria, Cameroon, and Gabon. Allen H. Godbey says that the Portuguese founded the island of San Thome in 1471. In the year 1484, King John II of Portugal, who reigned from 1481-1495, offered the Jews of his kingdom the choice of baptism or settling at San Thome. Multitudes of Jews were sent to this island during the reign of King John II.[21] These Jews, "Judeos" as the Portuguese called them, are serious, reserved and wealthy, holding most of the trade in their hands.

The Portuguese were the first Europeans to establish themselves on the west African coast. They came first as merchants, and secondly as conquerors and slavers. Later in this work, the black Jews in the Portuguese possessions in West Africa will be discussed in greater detail.

Now, let us return to the Jews of North Africa.

With the influx of tens of thousands of black Jews from Spain and Portugal seeking refuge in African ports, Morocco received a great share. But before this date many Jewish tribes were entrenched in Fez, the Atlas, and the desert. In Morocco there was a revival of Moorish and Jewish science in all areas. The Hebrew academy in Fez competed with the one in Kairuan, Algeria. There were many debates and lectures between the sages and scholars of these schools. Eldad, the Danite, a Hebrew from the Jewish kingdom of Ghana visited these schools in the ninth century.

There was a celebrated Hebrew college at Sijilmasa, in the desert, south of Fez. The school of Sijilmasa produced many illustrious scholars. There were grammarians, masters of Talmudic law, poets, and philologists.

This period of Jewish scholarship came to an end when the fanatical Almohades ("Unitarians") went on the warpath in 1145 and destroyed the city of Sijilmasa; this reign of terror was carried out against all non-Muslims. Concerning the destruction of Sijilmasa Ibn Ezra writes:

"I say, let there be mourning for the community of Sijilmasa, city of great scholars and sages; she sees her light covered with shadows; the pillars of the Talmuds were shattered; the temple of law was destroyed and the Mishnah was trodden under foot."

There are many Jewish tribes and settlements throughout Morocco and the Sahara Desert: The Ait Moussa, or Beni-Moussa, "Sons of Moses," is one of the spectacular Jewish tribes. Leo Africanus, a Moorish converted Jew, states that: "The Jews of North Africa are of a hybrid quality: They have proselytized and inter-married among the Greeks, Vandals, Romans, Spaniards, and Portuguese." The Jews

intermarried among the Greeks when the latter established
their colony in Libya called Cyrenaica; some intermarriages
occurred between Jews, Romans, and Vandals when the latter two invaded North Africa; and before the Jews were expelled from Spain and Portugal there were some intermarriages. Considering all this intermingling, many Jews of
North Africa still retain much of their colored features.
According to Maurice Fishburg (who was quoted by Allen
Godbey) he "was unable to distinguish a Jew from a Mohammedan while passing along the streets of Algiers, Constantine (a city of northern Africa), and Tunis. It is remarkable that among the non-Jewish natives there are seen many
Jews of Negroid type."[22]

Fishburg visited Africa during the early part of the twentieth century.

There are black Jews living in the multitude of oases
in the Sahara Desert. Nahum Slouschz, the white Jewish
rabbi, visited these Jews of North Africa and the Sahara
during the turn of this century. Slouschz obtained his information of these Jews from three sources: (1) from the
historical records of the Arabs, (2) from the oral traditions
of the inhabitants of the Sahara, (3) from archeological
evidence excavated from the ruins of old Jewish cities in
the Sahara and Sudan, which date from the thirteenth
century.

About half way down the eastern border of Algeria, there
are large settlements of black Jews at a place called Wargla,
says Slouschz. Jews were at Wargla as early as 620 A.D. according to Godbey. Again Godbey says "In the Wargla oasis
of Algeria, 350 miles from the Mediterranean, is a colony of
Jews 'as black as Negroes.' "

In the Gharian section of Libya, not too far from Wargla,
there exists the troglodyte Jews. It is reported that the Jews
fled to the strongholds of the Nefoussa mountain range because of Roman and Arab persecution. Godbey quotes H. S.
Cowper who says that the Jews of the city of Tripoli assert
that they migrated from Gharian. These Jews constructed

subterranean synagogues and underground houses. Slouschz visited the strongholds of these troglodyte Jews in the early part of this century. The Jews had built compartments three and four stories underground, containing a population of thirty thousand. Godbey says that: "Hesse-Wartegg visited their cities of Beni-Abbas, Jebel Nefussa, Yehud Abbas, Tigrena, Jebel Iffren." They had shops, stores, schools, and synagogues, all underground.

The achievements of these Jews prove what a persecuted society can do under adverse conditions. These Jews had a foundation to build on, unlike other persecuted people; they had their history, culture, laws, language, and skills.

Between Wargla and the Gharian, there is a Jewish town called Tigrena. Here, the Jews have also constructed subterranean compartments. Nahum Slouschz says he was guided to an ancient synagogue which was located underground; at this time he made an extensive observation of the village which contained twenty underground courts and its 700 inhabitants; also, he found there a young man teaching Hebrew.[23]

When Slouschz was in this city about one hour, the men had just returned from the market; Slouschz says they are "all of a fine, dark type." The rabbi was descended from Jews who had immigrated from Morocco.

The rabbi, at this time, informed Slouschz of the fact that there existed in the district many traces of deserted Jewish cities and cemeteries now abandoned. The Jews of this country have handed down the oral tradition that in ancient times they constituted the majority of the population but that epidemics, wars and frequent conversions to Islamism have reduced their number.[24] On one occasion Slouschz met a Jewish itinerant merchant of Nefoussa who had just arrived from Fezzan; this Jew had traveled all the routes of the Sahara; he assured Slouschz that other Jews existed at least in the east Sudan (Chad, Sudan, and Ethiopia), "A black-skinned population which some call the Felici and which are generally known among the Tauregs as the

Krit. They observe the Sabbath and are known to be of Jewish origin."[25]

Many of the tribes in the Sahara and in the Sudan are Moslems in religion but are Hebrew in nationality. Nahum Slouschz says: "Numbers of these Islamized Jews may be found everywhere." They are among the Nomads of Algeria, the Smul, the Hanansha, the Traras, the Masmata, the Mua-jerin, the Kabyles, the Tuat; you will find them among the Ureshfana, the Ghariani, the Brami in Tripoli; you will find them in southern Morocco among the powerful clans of the Daggatuns, who control the routes to the Sudan and southward. They are non-Jewish by religion but aware of their Hebrew origin. They are friendly to the Jewish merchants. Frequently the Jew is the only communication between these tribes and the outside world.[26]

The Daggatun Jews are scattered in clans through many caravan route oases of the Sahara and the Sudan. Godbey says the word Daggatun means traders; they are located near Timbuktu and hundreds of miles northward; they are also found east of Timbuktu and Gao.

The two main factors that motivated the black Jews to penetrate into North Africa were commerce and persecution; also, these two factors impelled them to migrate into central Africa which is known as the Sudan.

THE WEST AFRICAN JEWS DURING THE SLAVE TRADE

The black Jews who migrated to the Sudan from the North converged with the Jews migrating from the eastern Sudan to the countries of the Niger River. It is a known fact that the Jews and Judaism were in Africa fifteen hundred years before Islam and that everywhere the Arabs went the Jews were there. The black Jews guided the Arabs and Moors into Spain and acted as interpreters. When the Moslems came into the Sahara, they found the black Jews stationed on all the trade routes, and I can positively say that where Mohammedanism is currently prevailing in the Sudan, Judaism once had been dominant.

There is much proof, and still much more to be revealed by scholars, that there existed prior to the slave trade and subsequent to it many Jewish tribes, colonies, and kingdoms in West Africa:

The Moorish writer, Leo Africanus, informs us of the past existence of a medieval Hebrew state called Kamnuria or Kanuria; its two main cities were Kamnuri (obviously its capital) and Naghira; and this state was located north of the Senegal River. According to this Moorish Jew, this black African Hebrew state had vanished by his time. There are two reasons given for the ruin of this kingdom: (1) The intensive sandstorms of the Sahara Desert caused droughts and rendered the cities uninhabitable; (2) the migration of the Fulas or Fulbe toward the West. The Kanuri call the Fulas "Fellata"; these Fulas transmigrated the entire Sudan from the Nile to Senegal. The Kanuri Jews are now located in the central Sudan along trails hundreds of miles north, south, east and west of Lake Chad where they migrated from Senegal.[27]

It is the conclusion of some scholars that when the Jewish kingdom of Ghana fell, many of the Hebrew tribes established settlements among the African tribes throughout central and western Africa.[28]

Thus, the Moorish writer, Al Edrisi, of Andalusia, Spain, wrote in the early part of the twelfth century about the powerful Hebrew colony of Lamlam. Lamlam was situated about two hundred miles west of Timbuktu. The Hebrew merchants were then monopolizing the trade that was concentrated at Timbuktu. Lamlam was entirely Jewish and she fought wars to maintain her control of trade.[29]

Edrisi also said that there were only two towns south of the Kingdom of Ghana and continues: "According to what the people of this country report, the inhabitants are Jews." When they had reached the age of puberty they were branded on the countenance or at least on the temple with fire, leaving identifying marks. All the dwellings in their countries were built on the bank of a river, which flowed into the Nile.[30] Edrisi meant the Niger River. It was the belief of the time that the Niger formed an upper reach of the Nile.

The black African Hebrews had settlements not only in the interior of Africa; but they also had communities on the west coast of Africa from Morocco to Angola.

In the year 1856 Dr. J. L. Wilson wrote his history of western Africa: He transmits to us the composite religious culture of some of the inhabitants of Senegambia (or Senegal) and Guinea; in Senegal, he said, there "is a complete medley of paganism, Judaism, and Mohammedanism, and it is difficult to say which of the three occupies the most prominent place, or exerts the greatest influence upon the character of the people." However, the sentiment of the inhabitants regarding this multi-religious mixture was that the combination of the three religions furthered the welfare of all.

How do we rationalize and explain the medley of paganism, Judaism, and Mohammedanism near the ruins of the medieval Jewish kingdom of Kamnuria? It is obvious to researchers that after the break-up of the Hebrew kingdoms of Ghana, Kamnuria, and Lamlam, the black Jews migrated to remote regions of the interior and the coast; then these Hebrews came under the pressure of Moslem propaganda and pagan influence, resulting in what is known as "cultural diffusion." If you recall what Slouschz said, many Jews became Moslems but still retained their Jewish origin.

Wilson also informs us that in northern Guinea there is a conglomeration of Judaism and paganism combined, and in southern Guinea there is a combination of Judaism, paganism, and some traces of Christianity. In northern Guinea, or Portuguese Guinea, Judaism is more highly practiced; some of the outstanding rites are purifications, the observance of the new moons, a designated period of the weeping for the dead, during which time they wear sack cloths and ashes; bloody animal sacrifices, with the careful sprinkling of blood upon the door posts and the altars; the division of the tribes into different families, frequently into twelve parts (the twelve tribes of Israel); formal processions, circumcision, and various other practices, probably of Hebrew derivation. A few of these rituals, especially circumcision, might have been derived from the Moslems, but we are forced to consider the entire congeries of the Hebrew cultural traits which is indicative of the Hebrew religion.

Wilson says: "Although the natives of Africa retain these outward rites and ceremonies with the utmost tenacity, they have little or no knowledge of their origin, or the particular object which they are intended to commemorate. Many of them are performed to shield themselves from some threatened evil, or to secure some coveted good. But in the great majority of the cases they are attended merely as a matter of habit; and the only reason assigned for observing them is that their ancestors did the same before them."[31]

It stands to good reason that if their ancestors observed these Hebrew rites, they were surely Hebrews.

It is written: "They have said, come and let us cut them off from being a nation; that the name of Israel may be no more in their remembrance."[32]

Like the black Jews in America, some of the Jews of Guinea don't remember their original nationality. This deplorable ignorance is attributed to various causes: (1) The fall of the Hebrew kingdoms, (2) the lack of communication with Jewish educational centers (3) intense persecution, and the deliberate blotting out of the mind their true nationality. Thus, Nahum Slouschz said this about the Islamized Jews he met: "In most cases these Hebrews by race and Mussulmen by faith seek to hide their origin, which has become a burden to them." In another example, the persecution of the black Jews in Portugal was so ruthless and frequent that Cecil Roth[33] tells us the Jews did not divulge to their children the secret of their religion until they had attained the age of reason. The Hebrew religion is such that if you deny your religion, you will eventually deny your nationality. The sociologists and psychologists know, and history has proven that, if you deny your culture and nationality over a long period of time you will totally forget it through a process of assimilation.

The black Jews came to Africa not only by land but also by sea. As you recall, in the year 1484 King John of Portugal deported great numbers of black Jews to the African island of San Thome. The island of San Thome, near Nigeria and the Cameroon, was discovered by the Portuguese in 1471 and it was established as a penal colony; to this island Jews were sent who would not accept baptism. It is obvious that the Jews were deported to San Thome not only to mete out punishment to them; but King John's ulterior motive was to establish a commercial base with sophisticated black Jews in his growing empire in Africa. As time elapsed, the black Jews in Portugal and the black Jews in the Portuguese colonial possessions became known as "black Portuguese." They were called black Portuguese because they were born in Portugal and they knew the history, culture and language of Portugal.

As it has been mentioned before, King John[34] of Portugal furnished ships in order to deport the Jews to any country they desired; however, unscrupulous Portuguese captains exacted as much money as they could from the Jews and dumped their human cargo at various places along the west African coast. As a result, Allen Godbey writes that Winwoode Reade[35] met blacks in Guinea, West Africa, who called themselves Portuguese and claimed descent from Portugal; Reade wrote his book in 1864. In another case Daniel P. Mannix writes us that Captain Cutler, a slave trader from Boston, was "barbarously murdered, . . . with two of his sailors, by a community of black Portuguese established near the mouth of the Sierra Leone River."[36]

The Portuguese were the first Europeans to trade on the West African coast, and to establish colonies on a large scale: The Canary Islands were discovered by the Portuguese in

1341, ceded to Spain by Papal Bull in 1344; Senegal was discovered by the Portuguese in the fifteenth century, and the first settlements are believed to have been black Portuguese; the Gambia River mouth was discovered by the Portuguese in the fifteenth century; Sierra Leone first visited by the Portuguese in 1462; Guinea discovered by Portuguese in 1446; the island of San Thome discovered by Portuguese in 1471, the new inhabitants were black Jews deported here in 1484; black Jews migrated to the Angola coast from San Thome between 1484 and 1499; the white Portuguese missionaries reached Angola by 1560, but white settlers did not establish a community until 1575.

Let us return now to the Jews of San Thome Island. Scholars are uncertain concerning the exact number of Jews deported to this island; it is certain that the number lies in the thousands and perhaps the tens of thousands. Continuous research is needed in African Hebrew history, especially in the excavation of ruined Hebrew cities of Africa. When this gigantic work is completed, I believe the evidence will reveal information that will amaze humanity. It is my sincere belief that a greater number of black Jews were deported to the western coast of Africa than is admitted by some writers.

By the edict of King Manoel of Portugal in 1496 (banishing the Jews from Portugal), all Jews were to be out of Portugal by October 1497. However, considering this matter, he decided to Christianize the Jews, fearing the loss of a valuable population. He wanted the continued use of their knowledge and services. He concluded that the only way the Jews could be tolerated in his country was to force them into the Christian faith. In March 1497, a command was proclaimed throughout Portugal for all Hebrew children between four and fourteen years of age to be brought for baptism. All parents who did not bring their children voluntarily had their children taken away violently by the officials and forced into baptism. Cecil Roth writes:

"Scenes of indescribable horror were witnessed as they

were torn away by the royal bailiffs. The latter did not
obey their instructions too closely, frequently seizing young
people of both sexes up to the age of twenty. In many cases,
parents smothered their offspring in their farewell embrace.
In others, they threw them into wells in order to save them
from the disgrace of apostasy, and then killed themselves.
Sometimes, even old men were dragged to the churches and
forcibly baptized by over-zealous fanatics."[37]

Horrendous conditions like these (and much worse),
compelled many Jews to escape secretly out of the country.
These black Jews went to Portuguese colonial possessions in
western Africa.[38] Remember that the Portuguese colonies in
western Africa were Guinea, San Thome Island, Senegal,
Angola, and a few islands near the African coast. During the
persecutions in Portugal, thousands of Jews left the country.
The Jews were leaving the country in such large numbers
that in 1499 and 1531 the kings published a decree forbid-
ding the New Christians (black Jews) from leaving Portugal
without special permits.[39]

At this time many Jews became Christians out of fear;
many of them were known as secret Jews, practicing Judaism
in secret under the guise of Christianity. Some writers call
these Jews nominal Christians, Jews who are Christians in
name only, but practiced Judaism in secret.[40]

In spite of all the prejudices against the black Jews of
Portugal, they excelled in all the trades, skills, professions,
and businesses. The wealth of the Jews was tremendous.
Portugal is a small country about the size of the state of
Florida; nevertheless, in the year 1610, the Jews alone were
worth 80,000,000 ducats. The Jews dominated commerce
and the export trade; so naturally the black Jew would engage in commerce and trade in many parts of Africa, after
they had fled from Portugal.

THE BLACK JEWS OF ANGOLA

In the country called the Gabon near the Congo, there were black Jews known as the Bavumbu; some writers call them by various names such as Mavambo, Ma-Yomba, Mayumba, and Mavumbu. Abbe Proyart, a French writer, says that these Jews held the coast of Loango between the Congo River and Rio Muni in Gabon. In 1776 their country began about sixty miles from the coast and extended north from the Congo about two hundred miles. In appearance these black Jews are hardly distinguishable from the other Africans. It has been reported that these Jews practice some divination and magic like native Africans. However, they observe some Jewish ceremonies, and live in separate communities, not considering themselves native Africans. The villages of these Jews are situated along the Loango Coast for more than a hundred miles, even south of the Congo River. Godbey writes that when they are interrogated in regard to their origin, some of these Jews said they migrated from the south (probably Angola); some from the north (probably Nigeria); some from the other side of the mountains (perhaps Ethiopia). Like the Portuguese Jews, the Bavumbu Jews were very active in commerce.[41]

When David Livingstone was in Africa, he discovered a settlement of educated blacks about the year 1847; they were located inland about two hundred miles from the Loanda Coast, and are known as "the Jews of Angola." These black Jews were active in commerce, eager to learn, and possessed much knowledge of Portuguese history and law. In their commercial enterprises, these Jews penetrated inland hundreds of miles from the coast and were known also as clerks and writers. Livingstone[42] considered these Jews to be deportees from Portugal. St. Paul de Loanda began, like San Thome, as a penal colony for the punishment of criminals; in Portugal many of these black Jews were considered criminals. Also many of these black Jews of the land of

Angola, it is said, came from San Thome Island. All available evidence indicates that the Jews of the Angola coast were Portuguese Jewish outcasts.

Many black Jews were established inland and along the coast of Angola, the Congo, and Gabon. Friedrich Ratzel writes that the tribes on the Loango Coast and the Cabinda north of the Congo River were once Christianized. Ratzel observed a ceremony of baptism followed by circumcision. However, these tribes were Jewish in origin. The Christianity Ratzel saw among them was a disguise; the circumcision practiced among them is of Jewish derivation. The Christians in Portugal did not practice circumcision; in fact, Cecil Roth wrote that circumcision among Jews in Portugal was practically an impossibility; for its discovery was equal to a death sentence. Godbey wrote concerning the Mavumbu Jews on the Loango Coast:

"It seems that the Mavumbu may be the remnant of a much more numerous Judaism that was vigorously assailed by Portuguese missionaries. The Abbe Proyart records that nominal Christians (secret Jews) once numbered hundreds of thousands."[48]

Whenever the Jews were in Spain, Portugal, or their colonial possessions, they disguised themselves as Christians in outward form, but practiced Judaism in secret. Many of these new Christians knew Christian rites better than the old white Christians.

In the year 1547, the papal office authorized the establishment of the system of the Inquisition in Portugal; the word inquisition means inquiry or investigation. The Inquisition consisted of a tribunal of religious judges; its purpose was to investigate and purge out heretical Christians, persons who questioned certain Christian principles. Although some white Portuguese Christians suffered at the hands of the Inquisition, this system was mainly directed against the new Christians, the secret black Jews. The Inquisitions were persistent, gruesome, and ruthless in the totality of their procedures: They interfered in the private affairs of individuals; they intimidated and coerced individuals to inform on their neighbors; they employed a wide variety of continuous horrendous tortures, including public shows of burning human beings at the stake, and, in order to satisfy their desires for the punishment of heretics, they sought out not only the living, but also the dead.

Garcia d'Orta, a Jew of Portugal, was discovered to have been a secret Jew; his body was dug up out of his grave and burned by the Inquisition.[44]

In another case, a Jewish woman by the name of Elvira del Campo was indicted and tortured for two years in order to elicit a confession from her. The charges against her were not eating pork and putting on clean linen on Saturdays. According to this woman, these charges were not heretical practices, she wanted to be clean and pork made her sick.[45]

Whenever the Christian Jews could escape from Spain and Portugal beyond the reach of the Inquisition, they threw off the guise of Christianity and practiced Judaism openly, as they did in Turkey.[46] However, the unfortunate new Christians (nominal Christians, or secret Jews) in Portuguese possessions in western Africa, India, and elsewhere could not throw off the disguise of Christianity. The Inquisition even dispatched its Inquisitorial agents to the Canary Islands, Madeira, Guinea, India, South America, San Thome, and Angola in order to search out secret Jews. From 1561 to 1623 about 3,800 individuals were tried: many of them were Christian Jews of San Thome Island; they were charged with maintaining Jewish principles, Cecil Roth wrote that Christian Jews emigrated to the Portuguese colony of Angola in West Africa where agents of the Inquisition were sent to hunt them out in 1626.[47]

Now, we can understand why writers like Friedrich Ratzel considered the tribes along the Loango and Cabinda coast "Christians"; these Jews had to maintain a Christian guise and particularly so in the presence of white people. Any European could have been an agent of the Inquisition.

It is certain that many black Jews of Portugal, San

Thome, and Angola who became victims of the Inquisition and Portuguese persecution, were sold in the slave trade. This Atlantic slave trade lasted more than 400 years, from 1444 to about 1880 in some parts of South America.

Some scholars have located black Jews within the entire Niger River bend; the countries in this territory that have contained black African Jews include the following: Upper Volta, Ivory Coast, Ghana, Toga, Dahomey, and Nigeria. Joseph Dupuis,[48] concerning the Jews in 1824, says: "The lands occupied by these people cover a wide extent, between Massina and Kaby." Massina is located in southern Mali, inside the Niger River bend; and Kaby is found in the southern part of the Ivory Coast.

THE JEWS AMONG THE ASHANTEES

Among the Ashantees of the Gold Coast (Ghana) are found Jews who observe many Hebrew customs: They don't fight on Saturday but they rest. They celebrate the New Year of the Jews which occurs in September or early October; they used the word "Amen" at the end of their hymn of thanksgiving; like the Hebrews of old, they marry in their tribe only;[49] they perform cross-cousin marriages.[50] The Ashantee Jews also observe the laws of uncleanness after child-birth, purification ceremony of the fortieth day, the menstrual seclusion law,[51] and ceremonial ablutions. The Ashantee Jews have a breastplate like the High Priest in ancient Israel and it is divided into twelve parts, representing the twelve tribes of Israel.[52] Also, they have the misnefet or head-dress, with its gold disc in front which in ancient Israel bore an inscription—"Holy unto the Lord."[53]

THE BLACK JEWS OF DAHOMEY

Dr. J. Kreppel reported in 1926 that there existed a large Hebrew community of black Jews in the interior of Dahomey, West Africa. These Hebrews have their own central temple where they sacrifice animals. In their temple are found many laws engraved on tablets which are attached to the temple walls. They have a High Priest, with a large number of priestly families, whose members walk from house to house rendering educational and religious instructions to each family of the community. Moreover, these Jews have their own chumash (the five books of Moses) written on old parchment in Hebrew letters but they have no other books. What little Judaism they possess was transmitted to them from their ancestors. Dr. Kreppel says that they observe the Sabbath and other Jewish customs, despite the pressure from their pagan environment.[54]

YORUBA JEWS OF NIGERIA

There are black Jews in southern Nigeria who are called the "Emo Yo Quaim," or "Strange People," by the native Africans, but these black Jews call themselves by the Hebrew name "B'nai Ephraim" or "Sons of Ephraim." These Jews claim that their ancestors immigrated from Morocco, a fact which Godbey says is "supported by their language, a mixture of Maghrebi Arabic and local Negro speech. Thus *abu* ("father") has become *yaba,* umm ("mother"); Hebrew em is ima." Nevertheless, most of their language is similar to the black Yorubas around them. The Yorubas have influenced these Jews to a great extent in their external social life; it is said that the crocodile is the sacred animal for all; the customary sacrifices of the Yorubas appear to be the same for the Jews.

The assertion of these Yoruba Jews is that their ancestors were driven from locality to locality by Moslem persecution; they did not find rest even when they arrived at Timbuktu. Surely the prophecy has been fulfilled: "And among these nations shall thou find no ease, neither shall the sole of thy foot have rest: but the Lord shall give thee there a trembling heart, and failing of eyes, and sorrow of mind."[55] These Yoruba Jews lived in the Ondo district when Godbey wrote in 1930; this district is nine hundred miles southeast of Timbuktu. When Godbey wrote, they numbered about two thousand people in twenty small hamlets.

Pertaining to their Hebrew political structure and culture, they have seven hereditary heads of the community; their leadership is that of a priesthood. They are known to have copies of portions of the Torah (Old Testament) preserved in a "most holy place," however, their social life is not Torah-controlled like many of the Hebrew cultural traits among the Ashantee Jews. These black Jews observe certain Jewish customs, among which are the great holy days. In almost every way, these black Jews are like the Yorubas, and are hardly distinguishable from them, except for some outstanding Hebrew observances. One of the most notable among these black Jews was a young man named Bata Kindai Amgoza, ibn Lo Bagola, who was taken from Whydah, Dahomey, to Scotland. After he had received four years of the white man's education, he returned to his home in Africa.[56]

Dr. Allen H. Godbey postulates the position that black Jews were on the west African coast from Senegal to Angola and they, the Jews, were driven to this area from the Central Sudan by Moslem propagandism.[57] Having a knowledge of the black Jews in the United States, Dr. Godbey arrived at this conclusion:

"These facts have peculiar significance when the presence of Judaism among American Negroes is to be considered. Hundreds of thousands of slaves were brought to America from this Western Africa during the days of the traffic,[58] beginning nearly four hundred years ago. How much more of Judaism survived among West African Negroes in that earlier time? As persecuted communities, they were rather more in danger than other Negroes of being raided by war-parties and sold as slaves. It may be considered certain that many partially Judaized Negroes were among the slaves brought to America. How many of them might still hold some Jewish customs here is another question."[59]

Before Dr. Godbey published his book, *The Lost Tribes a Myth,* Rabbi Matthew organized a Hebrew congregation in 1918 and proclaimed that the black people of the United States and the West Indies are the original black Hebrews.[60]

There are hundreds of thousands of black African Hebrews scattered throughout the United States, not only in the urban areas, but also in the rural communities of this nation. With the revelation of ample historical evidence, the authenticity of these black Hebrews can no longer be questioned; however, in regard to the purity of their Judaism among some of these Jews, that is another issue.

CONCLUSION

According to biblical prophecy, the black Hebrews were supposed to have gone into slavery and captivity. Thus we read of the prophet Jeremiah saying: "Judah is gone into captivity because of affliction, and because of great servitude: she dwelleth among the heathen, she findeth no rest: all her persecutors overtook her between the straits."[61]

Prophecy is similar to history in one respect, that is, it repeats itself. Duality in prophecy has been recognized by many scholars.

As the historical evidences indicate, the black Hebrews were snatched from the west coast of Africa and sold into captivity. Jeremiah again says:

"For, lo, the days come, saith the Lord, that I will bring again the captivity of my people Israel and Judah, saith the Lord: and I will cause them to return to the land that I gave to their fathers, and they shall possess it.

"For it shall come to pass in that day, saith the Lord of hosts, that I will break his yoke from off thy neck, and will burst thy bonds, and strangers shall no more make him serve.

"But they (the Hebrews) shall serve the Lord their God, and David their king, whom I will raise up unto them.

"Therefore fear thou not, O my servant Jacob, saith the Lord; neither be dismayed, O Israel: for, lo, I will save thee from afar, and thy seed from the land of their captivity; and Jacob shall return, and shall be at rest and tranquil, and none shall make him afraid.

"For I am with thee, saith the Lord, to save thee: though I make a full end of all nations whither I have scattered thee, yet will I not make a full end of thee: but I will correct thee in measure, and will not leave thee altogether unpunished."[62]

"The valley of dry bones" spoken of by the prophet Ezekiel represents the nations that hold the black Hebrews under slavery and oppression, and the dry bones represent the black Hebrews. Ezekiel says:

"So I prophesied as he commanded me, and the breath came into them,[63] and they lived, and stood up upon their feet, an exceeding great army.

"Then he said unto me, son of man, these bones are the whole house of Israel: behold, they say, our bones are dried, and our hope is lost: we are cut off.

"Therefore prophesy and say unto them, Thus saith the Lord God; Behold I will open your graves,[64] and cause you to come up out of your graves[65] and bring you into the land of Israel."

The prophet Ezekiel calls the country wherein the black Hebrews are oppressed, "graves."

"And ye shall know that I am the Lord, when I have opened your graves, O my people, and brought you up out of your graves.

"And shall put my spirit in you, and ye shall live, and I shall place you in your own land: then shall ye know that I the Lord have spoken it, and performed it, saith the Lord."[66]

Epilogue

At the time that I am writing these pages, Rev. Ralph Abernathy is traveling around the country telling the American people: "I am going to Washington to tell the Pharaohs to let my people go." As it was with the Pharaohs of ancient Egypt, so it is unlikely that the leaders in Washington will concede to the demands of the Poor People's March.

Considering all the rampant violence in the United States, there are many indications that the March on Washington will erupt into violence. The power structure concedes nothing without a demand. When the government refuses to effect reforms, and to implement justice, the people lose respect for the institutions of "law and order"; law and order without justice are worthless in a democracy. When peaceful demonstrations do not soften the attitude of the government, militant and vigorous tactics must be employed by the militants in order to prevail upon the government; these tactics sometimes come close to anarchy. At this tense point, a mass movement can travel in one of two directions: If the government concedes to the demands of the people "all well and good"; the mass movement falls apart because it has accomplished its objective. On the other hand, if the government refuses the demands of the mass movement, it generally suppresses the rebellion or civil disobedience. When the people continue to rebel and the government continues to suppress, this condition leads to fascism and a dictatorship. There follows mass murder, which is committed in the name of law and order.

Dr. Martin Luther King expressed these thoughts before he was assassinated: "If conditions do not change soon in this country, we will have a fascist police state in the 1970s. I don't think that America has the moral strength and will to resolve her racial problem and to avert a fascist take-over; but if rapid, collective, constructive action is taken immediately, we can save the American cities from disaster. If a police state is established in America, this will fulfill the prophecy of Daniel: 'And at that time shall Michael stand up, the great prince which standeth for the children of thy people: and there shall be a time of trouble, such as never was since there was a nation even to that same time: and at that time thy people shall be delivered, every one that shall be found written in the book.' " (Dan. 12:1).

Notes

CHAPTER I

1. This point will be proven later.
2. Consult Rashi's *Commentary on Genesis.*
3. There were two Ethiopian nations: one in eastern Africa, as we know of it today, and the other Ethiopia was situated near the Persian Gulf in the Garden of Eden.
    Read *The Life and Works of Josephus.* Philadelphia: Toronto: The John C. Winston Company, 1957, p. 41.
4. The people in Philadelphia, Pennsylvania, call themselves Philadelphians, not Englishmen or Italians, etcetera.
5. Gen. 11:1-9.
6. Dr. Speiser.
7. Gen. 2:11.
8. *See* Dr. Speiser's *Commentary on Genesis,* footnote seven, p. 67.
9. *Bible Dictionary,* William Smith.
10. The phrase, "Garden of Eden," means pleasure or paradise.
11. *Bible Dictionary,* William Smith. Philadelphia: 1948, p. 155, *(see* the word *Eden).*
12. Herbert Wendt, a German writer says: "All indications point to the fact that Asia was the cradle of the black race." *It Began in Babel.* New York: Delta Dell Publishing Co., 1964, p. 368.
13. For more information about the Sumerians read *It Began in Babel,* Herbert Wendt. New York: Delta Dell Publishing Company, 1964, pp. 78-96.

CHAPTER II

1. Gen. 9:19.
2. Gen. 8:14.
3. Gen. 11:1-8.
4. Gen. 10:8, and read *The Life and Works of Flavius Josephus,* The John C. Winston Co., Philadelphia: p. 39.
5. John Clark Ridpath, *Universal History,* Vol. II. New York: The Jones Brothers Publishing Co., 1897, p. 412.
6. *Ibid.,* p. 413.

7. Herbert Wendt, *It Began in Babel*. New York: 1964, p. 89.
8. Cf. the *Columbia Encyclopaedia*, third edition, 1963 (*see* the word race), p. 1757.
9. Cf. the *Encyclopaedia of Social Science*, Macmillan Company, Vol. 1-11, p. 605. New York.
10. Cf. the word caucasian in the *Shorter Oxford English Dictionary*, vol. 1, p. 278.
11. Herbert Wendt, *It Began in Babel*. New York: Delta Dell Publishing Company, 1964, pp. 403-405.
12. *See* the word race in the *Columbia Encyclopaedia*, third edition, 1963, p. 1757.
13. *Introduction to Anthropology*. Beals and Hoyer, 2nd ed., pp. 103-105.
14. *Story of Man*. Coon, New York: 1954, p. 209.
15. Ex. 4:6-7.
16. Lev. 13:10-11, 13:19-20, 13:26-27, 13:43-44.
17. Lev. 13:46.
18. Lev. 13:45.
19. Read Num. 12:1-12.
20. Read Ex. 12:1-12.
21. Num. 12:2.
22. Ex. 4:6.
23. II Kings 5:1-27.

CHAPTER III

1. Herbert Wendt, *It Began in Babel*. New York: Delta Dell Publishing Company, 1964, p. 79.
2. *Ibid.*, p. 85.
3. *See* Chapter II.
4. Gen. 10:6 and 10:15-20.
5. In ancient times there was an ancestral and political relationship between the black people of Ethiopia, Egypt, and the Canaanites.
6. From slavery, Moses led the children of Israel out of the land of Egypt; and Joshua brought the children of Israel into the land of Canaan. (Josh. 1:6 and 3:10.)
7. Gen. 10:15.
8. Flavius Josephus, *The Life and Works of Flavius Josephus*. Philadelphia: Toronto: The John C. Winston Co., 1957, p. 266.
9. Herbert Wendt. *It Began in Babel*. New York: Delta Dell Publishing Company, 1964, pp. 93, 94.
10. *Ibid.*, p. 93.
11. Read Gen. 10:15-18.
12. Dr. William Chomsky, *Hebrew the Eternal Language*. Philadelphia: The Jewish Publication Society of America, 1957, p. 34.

13. Gen. 12:1-6.
14. *See* the word *Canaanite.* William Smith, L.L.D., *Bible Dictionary.* Philadelphia: The John C. Winston Co., 1948, p. 103.
15. Read Gen. 10:6 "The Sons of Ham: Cush (Ethiopia) and Mizraim (Egypt), and Phut (Somaliland to Senegal) and Canaan." Dr. Allen H. Godbey, Ph.D. said, Mizraim is Egypt and Phut is Somaliland (including central and west Africa).
    The Lost Tribes a Myth. Durham, No. Carolina: Duke University Press, 1930, pp. 23 and 256 (see map).
16. William Chomsky, *Hebrew the Eternal Language.* Philadelphia: Jewish Publication Society, 1957, p. 25.
17. Read the *Babylonian Talmud* by Rabbi Dr. I. Epstein, section called "Sanhedrin," Volume II. London: The Soncino Press, 1935, pp. 608-609.
18. *Collier's Encyclopaedia* Vol. III. Great Britain: Crowell Collier & Macmillan, Inc., 1967, p. 47.
19. Herbert Wendt, *It Began in Babel.* New York: Delta Dell Publishing Company, 1964, p. 94.
20. The word *Punic* means Phoenician.
21. *See* the word *Mizraim* in the *Bible Dictionary* by William Smith, L.L.D. Philadelphia: The John C. Winston Co., 1948, p. 411.
22. Allen H. Godbey, Ph.D., *The Lost Tribes a Myth.* Durham, North Carolina: Duke University Press, 1930, pp. 23, 94, 694, 695.
23. Edgerton and Carpenter, *Elementary Algebra.* Pp 11, 12.
24. Gen. 10:13-14.
25. *See* the word Philistine in the *Bible Dictionary* by William Smith, L.L.D. Philadelphia: The John C. Winston Company, 1948, p. 513. (*See* also, *It Began in Babel,* H. Wendt, p. 12.)
26. Herbert Wendt, *It Began in Babel.* New York: Delta Dell Publishing Company, 1964, p. 13.
27. *Ibid.,* p. 11.
28. *Ibid.,* p. 13.
29. *Ibid.*

CHAPTER IV

1. This particular point will be proven later.
2. Gen. 11:10-32.
3. Ishmael was the father of the Arabs and Ishmael's mother was an Egyptian. Gen. 16:1-11.
4. *The Life and Works of Flavius Josephus.* Philadelphia: Toronto: The John C. Winston Company, 1957, p. 48. Read Gen. 25:12.
5. Gen. 42:30.
6. Read Gen. 38:1 and Judg. 3:5-6.
7. P. 368.

8. Down through the ages, the scholars have agreed that the Hamites belong to the African family of nations. The Hamites are listed in Geneiss 10:6-20.

9. Judg. 3:5-6, Gen. 38:2-3. Solomon, also, takes an African woman to be his wife (the daughter of Pharaoh, the king of Egypt). I Kings 3:1.

10. Allen H. Godbey, Ph.D., *The Lost Tribes a Myth*. Durham, North Carolina: Duke University Press, 1930, p. 158.

11. Herbert Wendt, *It Began in Babel*. New York: Delta Dell Publishing Company, 1964, p. 14.

12. Solomon Grayzel, *A History of the Jews*. Philadelphia: The Jewish Publication Society, 1947, p. 42.

13. Israel Abraham, *Jewish Life in the Middle Ages*. Philadelphia: Jewish Publication Society and Meridian Books, 1958, pp. 98, 99.

14. J. A. Rogers, *World's Great Men of Color*. New York: Futuro Press, Inc., 1947, p. 124.

15. William Smith, L.L.D., *Bible Dictionary*. Philadelphia: The John C. Winston Company, 1948, p. 611. *See* the word *Sheba*.

16. *Ibid.,* p. 819, Map I. The Cushites who are the descendants of Ham are shown in yellow.

17. Joseph J. Willams, S.J., Ph.D. *Hebrewism of West Africa*. New York: The Dial Press, 1930, p. 160.

18. Daniel P. Mannix, *Black Cargoes*. New York: The Viking Press, p. 242. Also *see Collier's Encyclopaedia*. Crowell, Collier and Macmillan, Inc., 1967, p. 75.

19. I Kings 10:1.

20. The Queen of Sheba was known to the Arabians by the name of Bilkis. Herbert Wendt, *It Began in Babel*. New York: Delta Dell Publishing Company, 1964, p. 107. Also *see:* J. A. Rogers' *World's Great Men of Color*. New York: Futuro Press, Inc., 1947, p. 35.

21. J. A. Rogers says: At this time Arabia was part of the Sedan or Sudan Empire. This empire included Upper Egypt (known as the Sudan today), Ethiopia, and parts of Arabia. *Ibid.,* p. 35.

22. *The Life and Works of Flavius Josephus*. Philadelphia and Toronto: The John C. Winston Co., 1957, pp. 252, 253.

23. Throughout their long history, the Ethiopians more than once conquered Egypt. When Moses was in Egypt, he was appointed to the status of a general to expel the Ethiopians. *Ibid.,* pp. 77, 78.

24. *The Life and Works of Flavius Josephus,* on page 264, relates the following: Zerah, the Ethiopian, came to fight against Asa (the King of Judah) ; this event took place about 941 B.C. Asa defeated the Ethiopians at Mareshah. This advance of the Ethiopians into the land of Israel was a great indication of the emerging power of the Ethiopian Empire at this period. Josephus relates that Shishak or Sheshonk, the first King of the Bubastite Dynasty (the Libyan Dynasty), had mostly Libyans and Ethiopians in his army. There appears to have existed some kind of

politcal-miltary alliance between the Libyan kings of Egypt and the Ethiopians. Basil Davidson, author of *The Lost Cities of Africa,* pp. 216, 218, and Professor Allen H. Godbey, author of *Lost Tribes a Myth,* p 866 (see map), support the fact that the Habashites (Abyssinians or Ethiopians) were originally inhabitants of Arabia. The scholars are doubtful of the path of march of Zerah's army; but I believe that he marched from Arabia, not Egypt, because of the many Ethiopians living in Arabia. We must remember that Arabia was part of the Ethiopian Empire and Josephus calls the Queen of Sheba the Queen of Egypt (Upper Egypt) and Ethiopia. Moreover, Josephus calls Zerah the King of the Ethiopians. If Asa had not stopped Zerah at Mareshah, it is highly probable that the Ethiopians would have succeeded the Twenty-second Bubastite (Libyan Kings 941 B.C.) Dynasty in Egypt. Because the Ethiopians were vanquished by Asa, they did not become great in the international arena until the year 712 B.C. At this time the Twenty-fifth Dynasty (Ethiopian) was established in Egypt, and Ethiopia became a world power. *See Webster's Biographical Dictionary,* the word *Taharka,* p. 1441.

25. J. A. Rogers, *World's Great Men of Color.* New York: Futuro Press, Inc., 1947, pp. 31, 35.

26. Joseph J. Williams, Ph.D., *Hebrewism of West Africa.* New York: The Dial Press, 1930, pp. 160, 161.

26. The capitals of many nations have been changed from one place to another: The capital of ancient Israel was changed from Hebron to Jerusalem. The capital of colonial United States was established in three places in turn: New York, Philadelphia, and Washington, D.C.

27. *See* the word *Aksum* in *Webster's Geographical Dictionary,* p. 17.

28. Basil Davidson, *Africa: History of a Continent.* New York: The Macmillan Company, 1966, p. 53.

29. Himyar was a city state along the coast of the Red Sea in southern Arabia.

30. *Habesh* means Abyssinia. Abyssinia is a Portuguese corruption of the Arab "El Ha be sha" (*See* the word *Ethiopia* in *Webster's Geographical Dictionary*) . The Habeshians, from *Habesh,* were not Semites, but Cushites. (*See* Basil Davidson's, *The Lost Cities of Africa.* Boston: Toronto: Little, Brown and Company, 1959, p. 218.) The Habeshians descended from the Cushites, and they migrateid from the Persian Gulf. Immigrating into Arabia, they eventually crossed the Red Sea into Africa and became known to modern man as Abyssinians or Ethiopians.

31. Allen H. Godbey, *The Lost Tribes a Myth.* Durham, N. C., Duke University Press, 1930, p. 181.

32. *Ibid.,* pp. 182, 183, 185.

33. The Habashan or Habashites (Abyssinians) "they who would found Axum after centuries of Sabaean and other Arabian infiltration and invasion—appear in early inscriptions of the eighteenth dynasty

(1580-1350 B.C.) which tells of trade with the land of Punt." Basil Davidson, *Lost Cities of Africa*. Boston: Little, Brown and Company, 1959, p. 216.

34. Dhu Nuwas' Hebrew name was Joseph.

35. These were black Christians.

36. The vandals crossed the Mediterranean Sea into Africa.

37. The Moslems ruled Spain and Portugal, and they penetrated parts of France.

38. Joseph Gaer, *How the Great Religions Began*. New York: and Toronto: The New American Library, 1956, p. 194.

39. The sociologist, Alvin L. Bertrand, postulates four stages of a mass movement. In addition, he postulates a stage of formal organization into a bureaucratic structure. See *Basic Sociology*, New York: Meredith Publishing Company, 1967, p. 136.

40. Dan. 8:15. Gabriel appeared unto Daniel after the destruction of the First Temple, 586 B.C.

41. Read Edward Gibbon, *The Decline and Fall of the Roman Empire, II*. New York: The Modern Library, 1931, p. 653.

42. Gen. 21:18.

43. Read Erwin I. J. Rosenthal, *Judaism and Islam*. London: New York: Thomas Yoseloff, 1961, pp. 3-47.

44. *Ibid.*, p. 24.

CHAPTER V

1. Gen. 10:6. Ham had four sons, Cush, Mizraim, Phut, and Canaan. The Land of Ham connotates Egypt and the continent of Africa, Psa. 78:51, 105:23, 106:22.

2. *It Began in Babel*. New York: Dell Publishing Company, 1964 p. 66.

3. *See* the name *Blumenbach* in *Webster's Biographical Dictionary*.

4. Obviously, the words *Ophren* and *Apher* are the same. In listing the progeny of Abraham and Keturah, the bible employs the word *Apher* in Genesis 25:4. However, Josephus uses *Ophren* which is a latinized counterpart of the word *Apher*. We must remember that Josephus lived and wrote in Rome. Now, the modern Latin spelling of Africa is *Afer*. For reference, see the word *Afro* in *Webster's Dictionary*. The word *Afer* in the Hebrew, Aramaic and Phoenician-Carthagian languages means dust or earth, which carries a connotation of blackness. The early Romans knew that the Libyans were black people. They most probably knew, also, that the word *Afer* meant darkness. Hence, the nickname for Africa is the "Dark Continent" which was given to Africa by the Europeans.

5. *The Life and Works of Josephus*, 1957 edition, translated by William Whiston. Philadelphia: Toronto: The John C. Winston Company, 1957, p. 50.

6. The ancient Egyptians were a black-skinned race. All available evidence supports this fact. Any disposition or attempt to classify the Egyptians as a Caucasoid race is to be considered as a white supremacy fallacy, depriving the black races of their heritage in order to glorify the white race. Most statues and pictures of the ancient Egyptian gods and kings depict black qualities, the thick lips and broad noses. Paul Hamlyn, *Egyptian Mythology*. London: Westbook House, 1965, pp. 7-147. The Greek historian, Herodotus, says the Egyptians are black-skinned. Herodotus traveled throughout Egypt. *The History of Herodotus*, translator, George Rawlinson. New York: Tudor Publishing Company, 1941, p. 115.

7. The Canaanites in Africa. See Allen H. Godbey, *The Lost Tribes a Myth*. Durham, N. C.: Duke University Press, 1930, p. 206.

8. For Bradley and Norden's reports see Joseph J Williams, *Hebrewism of West Africa*, 2nd ed. New York: The Dial Press, 1931, p. 184.

9. The Egyptians called their country Khemi or Chem "the black Land." From this word we get the words alchemy and chemistry. Godbey, *Works*. Durham, N. C.: 1930, p. 22.

10. *World's Great Men of Color*. New York: Futuro Press, Inc., 1947, p. 1.

11. *The History of Herodotus*, translated by George Rawlinson. New York: Tudor Publishing Co., 1941, p. 108.

12. *Ibid.*, p. 96.

13. For detailed information on the gods of Egypt, *see* Paul Hamlyn, *Egyptian Mythology*. London: Westbook House, 1965.

14. The Amorites are not Semites as many prejudiced scholars assert, but they were Hamites, the descendants of Ham through Canaan. (Gen. 10:6 and 10:15-16.)

15. *History of Assyria*. New York: London: Charles Scribner's Sons, 1923, p. 31.

16. From the year 2000-1500 B.C., the continent of Europe and the Middle East, as far as India, underwent a radical migratory transformation. The descent of the Indo-Europeans or Indo-Germans is established from a common ancestor (one that is the descendant from Japheth) probably in eastern Europe. The prehistoric dialects of the Indo-Europeans accompanied their migrations into the western borders of Europe, Italy, Greece, Iran, Assyria (now extinct), Persia, and India.

When we say that an individual is Indo-European, we mean Indo-Aryan. Many people from India are Indo-Aryan. The prefix "Indo" means Indian, and the word "Aryan" in the strict meaning stands for upper class or caste. In the Aryan and Nazi philosophy the Aryan or Germanic race is supposed to be the superior race or caste. Therefore, when the Aryans came to India they established their race as the superior one. As a result, the caste system came into practice among the black native Indians. The Aryan race is supposed to be the pure race (according to Nazi and Aryan philosophy), however, they have mixed their blood with every people from the Pillars of Hercules to India.

17. *It Began in Babel.* New York: Dell Publishing Company, Inc., 1961, pp. 90-91.

18. This form of brutality, nationalist fervor, and censorship was instituted in Hitler's Nazi Germany, Napoleon's Imperial France, Stalin's Communist Russia, Franco's Fascist Spain, and Mussolini's Fascist Italy, during or after a state of disorder: The Reign of Terror, The French and Spanish revolutions, The Great Purge, and the riots. Immediately thereafter, dictatorships were established in all of the above countries. The American people must be alert in order to see that it does not happen here. The black riots can be averted by rapid constructive reforms.

19. Ex. 1:11-16. The decree to destroy the Hebrew males has its parallel in the American society; the black male suffers more than the black female.

20. This woman is undoubtedly the same Ethiopian woman mentioned in Numbers 12:1.

21. Much of the information in this book about Moses cannot be found in the Bible, but it can be found n the *Life and Works of Josephus,* translated by William Whiston. Philadelphia: Toronto: The John C. Winston Company, 1957, pp. 77-78. Flavius Josephus was a member of the royal priestly family in Jerusalem. He was at Jerusalem when the city was destroyed by the Romans. He was educated in the politics of his nation and learned the religion and history of his people. Josephus, obviously, had the availability of the vital historical records (other than the Bible) which were contained in the temple archives in Jerusalem.

22. The word "Ethiopia" is a Greek word that means dark skin or burnt faces; the Ethiopians in the highlands called themselves Abyssinians.

23. Harold Lamb, *Cyrus the Great.* New York: Doubleday and Company, Inc., 1960, p. 247.

24. *Story of Nations.* New York: Henry Holt and Company, 1952, p. 13.

25. For more information about the Axumite kingdom in Abyssinia, *see* Chapter Four. Also *see* Basil Davidson, *The Lost Cities of Africa.* Boston: Toronto: Little, Brown and Company, 1959, pp. 25-50.

26. Ezion-geber is Israel's southern port that leads through the Gulf of Aqabah, which eventually enters into the Red Sea. The dispute over the use of this body of water led to the Arab-Israeli War of June, 1967.

27. There is a dissident viewpoint that the land of Ophir is in Arabia or India.

28. *The Life and Works of Josephus,* translated by William Whiston. Philadelphia: Toronto: The John C. Winston Company, 1957, pp. 252-253.

29. When Josephus says that the Queen of Sheba is queen of Egypt and Ethiopia, by "Egypt" he obviously means Upper Egypt (the southern portion of the Egyptian empire). During the reign of the Twentieth Dynasty of Egypt, the empire declined rapidly. Ramses IV-XII, these Ramessides reigned from 1167 to 1090 B.C., all weaklings.

Because of the weaknesses of the Twentieth and Twenty-first Dynasties, Ethiopian troops penetrated into southern Egyptian territory, giving some Egyptian dominion to the Queen of Ethiopia.

30. *Ibid.*, p. 78.

31. *See* Chapter Four.

32. *See* Josephus' *Works*, p. 261.

33. *Hebrewism of West Africa*. New York: The Dial Press, 1930, p. 184, footnote 100.

34. *The Lost Tribes a Myth*. Durham, North Carolina: Duke University Press, 1930, p. 201.

35. Cities of refuge, Num. 35:11.

36. Williams, *Works*, New York: 1930, p. 169.

37. For race mixing see Harold Lamb, *Cyrus the Great*. New York: Doubleday and Company, Inc., 1960, p. 262.

38. For wide extent of Judaism, *see: Lost Tribes a Myth*. Durham, North Carolina: Duke University Press, 1930, p. 217.

39. The Barbary States are the countries extending from Egypt to the Atlantic Ocean; so called because the Romans considered the people here to be barbarians, hence, Berbers.

40. *See:* Solomon Grayzel, *A History of the Jews*, 8th Edition. Philadelphia: The Jewish Publication Society of America, 1956, p. 250.

41. *Ibid.*, pp. 302-303.

42. Nahum Slouschz, *Travels in North Africa*. Philadelphia: The Jewish Publication Society of America, 1927, p. 232.

43. Slouschz, works, p. 104.

44. *Ibid.*, p. 344.

45. *Ibid.*

46. *Hebrewism of West Africa*, 2nd Ed. New York: The Dial Press, 1930, p. 336 (see map).

47. There was a large Jewish colony at Elephantine before 525 B.C. *Ibid.*, p. 342.

48. Professor A. H. Godbey writes that the "Jewish Kingdom of Ghanata [or Ghana] was founded 300 A.D. by "white Libyans" [Berbers]."

As much as I admire Godbey for his monumental work, *Lost Tribes a Myth*, Durham, North Carolina: Duke University Press, 1930, p. 256, see map, I must disagree with him when he says that the founders of the Jewish kingdom of Ghanata were "white Libyans [Berbers]." Endeavoring to tell some truths, and at the same time trying not to render too much credit to the black races, Godbey contradicts himself: "White Libyan dynasty founded among the Negro Sonrhai about 620

A.D. by Za el Yemeni. . . . Za came from Wargla in southern Algeria. At this time all Jews in North Africa were colored. If you trace or look for Wargla on the map mentioned above, you will discover, in particular, that the words "black Jew" is written under the word Wargla (remember. Za came from Wargla).

Godbey was professor of the Old Testament in Duke University, Durham, North Carolina. He knew the entire truth about the black Jews, but he considered it unwise to reveal everything. Godbey was writing primarily to a white southern audience in 1930. At this time the Ku Klux Klan was in its heyday, and he did not want any repercussions. Moreover, if Godbey had said positively that the Za Dynasty and the original Jews were black, the power structure and the clergy would have come down on him like a storm.

Also, Heinrich Barth says that the kingdom of Ghana, or Ghanata was founded by Wakayamagha (Davidson says that Kayamagha was a title of the kings of Ghana) about 300 A.D. by a family of whites (Leucaethiopes? Fulbe?). The word *Leucaethiopes* means white Ethiopians. When European writers speak of white Asians or white Ethiopians, they are referring to black people who have thin faces, straight noses, and thin lips. Caucasian features are found among many black Africans. Concerning Barth's works see *Travels and Discoveries in North and Central Africa*, Volume III, London: Frank Cass and Company, Ltd., 1965, p. 657.

49. *See* Nahum Slouschz, *Travels in North Africa*. Philadelphia: The Jewish Publication Society of America, 1927, p. 344.

50. For Jewish kings *see:* Allen H. Godbey, *The Lost Tribes a Myth*. Durham, North Carolina: Duke University Press, 1930, p. 256, see map.

51. *See: Hebrewism of West Africa* 2nd ed. New York: The Dial Press, 1930, p. 227.

52. *Ibid.*, 228-229. Also *see:* Solomon Grayzel's *A History of the Jews*, 8th ed. Philadelphia: The Jewish Publication Society of America, 1947, p. 279.

53. *Travels in North Africa*. Philadelphia: The Jewish Publication Society of America, 1927, p. 345.

54. Obviously, Za Kasi was the fifteenth Za prince calculated from the year 790, because forty-four kings had already reigned by 790 A.D.

55. *Africa: History of a Continent.* New York: The Macmillan Company, 1966, pp. 150-155.

56. Basil Davidson, *The Lost Cities of Africa*. Boston/Toronto: Little, Brown and Company, 1959, p. 84.

57. The law that only a Moslem could be king was probably instituted by the Almoravid Moslem invader Abu Bakr.

58. Heinrich Barth, *Travels and Discoveries in North and Central Africa*, vol. III. London: Frank Cass and Company, Ltd., 1965, p. 659.

59. For the mosque of Timbuktu and Sankore *see:* Heinrich Barth's

Travels and Discoveries in North and Central Africa, vol. III. London: Frank Cass and Company, 1965, p. 662. For University of Sankore *see:* J. A. Rogers' *World's Great Men of Color*. New York: Futuro Press Inc., 1947, p. 133.

60. Barth, *Works* III. London: 1965, p. 663.

61. *Ibid.*, p. 665. For the change of the name of the Za Dynasty to the Sonni *see:* Basil Davidson's *Africa: History of a Continent*. New York: The Macmillan Company, 1966, p. 117.

62. Allen H. Godbey, *Lost Tribes a Myth*. Durham, North Carolina: Duke Unievrsity Press, 1930, p. 256, see map.

CHAPTER VI

1. *The History of Herodotus*, translated by George Rawlinson. New York: Tudor Publishing Company, 1941, pp. 256-263.

2. *Ibid.*, pp. 86, 263.

3. *Ibid.*, p. 115.

4. Walata was a city south of the Sahara not too far from the Niger River.

5. *Travels and Discoveries in North and Central Africa*, volume III. London: Frank Cass and Company, Ltd., 1965, p. 696.

6. *Hebrewism of West Africa*, 2nd ed. New York: The Dial Press, 1931, p. 303.

7. *Ibid.*, p. 290.

8. *See:* Herbert Wendt's *It Began in Babel*. New York: Dell Publishing Company, Inc., 1961, p. 13.

9. Shabat 18.

10. Babylonian Talmud, Sanhedrin 91a.

11. Onomastica Sacra.

12. Nahum Slouschz, *Travels in North Africa*. Philadelphia: The Jewish Publication Society of America, 1927, p. 337.

13. Allen H. Godbey, *The Lost Tribes a Myth*. Durham, North Carolina: Duke University Press, 1930, p. 207.

14. Slouschz, *Works*. Philadelphia: 1927, p. 228.

15. *Travels in North Africa*. Philadelphia: The Jewish Publication Society of America, 1927, p. 365.

16. Edward Gibbon, *The Decline and Fall of the Roman Empire*. New York: The Modern Library, 1931, p. 772.

17. L. B. Rogers, T Adam, W. Brown, *Story of Nations*. New York: Henry Holt and Company, 1952, p. 354.

18. Cecil Roth, *A History of the Marranos*, 2nd rev. ed. Philadelphia: The Jewish Publication Society of America, 1959, pp. 54, 55, 199.

19. *Work of Spinoza*. New York: Dover Publishing Company, 1951, see: Introduction—xix.

20. Roth, *Works*. Philadelphia: 1959, p. 55.

21. *Lost Tribes a Myth*. Durham, North Carolina: Duke University Press, 1930, p. 246.

22. *Ibid.*, p. 219. Also *see:* Nahum Slouschz, *Travels in North Africa*. Philadelphia: The Jewish Publication Society of America, 1927, pp. 351, 352, 353.

23. *Ibid.*, p. 134: (Slouschz).

24. *Ibid.*, p. 135.

25. Slouschz, *Works*. Philadelphia: 1927, p. 145.

26. *Ibid.*, p. 111 Also *see:* Solomon Grayzel, *A History of the Jews*, 8th ed. Philadelphia: The Jewish Publication Society of America, 1947, p. 729.

27. Leo Africanus, or Hassan ibn Mohammed el Wazzan el Zayyati, wrote a book called *History and Description of Africa* (Trans. Pory, 1600). Hakluyt Society, 1896.

Allen H. Godbey wrote about the Jewish Kingdom of Kamnuri in: *The Lost Tribes a Myth*. Durham, North Carolina: Duke University Press, 1930, pp. 223, 226, 242.

28. Joseph Williams, *Hebrewism of West Africa*, 2nd ed. New York: The Dial Press, 1931, p. 254.

29. Godbey, *Works*. Durham, North Carolina: 1930, pp. 223, 242.

30. Williams, *Works*. New York: 1931, p. 234.

31. Allen H. Godbey, *The Lost Tribes a Myth*. Durham, North Carolina: Duke University Press, 1930, p. 243.

32. Psa. 83:4.

33. *A History of the Marranos*, 2nd rev. ed. Philadelphia: The Jewish Publication Society of America, 1959, p. 358.

34. *Ibid.*, p. 55.

35. *See: Savage Africa*. New York: 1864. Also Godbey, *Works*. Durham, North Carolina: 1930, p. 251.

36. *Black Cargoes*. New York: The Viking Press, 1962, p. 162.

37. *A History of the Marranos*, 2nd rev. ed. Philadelphia: The Jewish Publication Society of America, 1959, p. 57.

38. *Ibid.*, pp. 394, 395, 78.

39. *Ibid.*, pp. 63, 69.

40. *Ibid.*, pp. 77, 205, 223, 385.

41. Friedrich Ratzel, *The History of Mankind*, Vol. III. New York: Macmillan and Company, 1898, p. 134.

42. *Travels and Researches in South Africa*. pp. 414, 479. *See* also: Allen H. Godbey, *Lost Tribes a Myth*. Durham, North Carolina: Duke University Press, 1930, p. 252.

43. Godbey, *Works*. Durham, North Carolina: 1930, p. 250.

44. Cecil Roth, *A History of the Marranos*, 2nd rev. ed. Philadelphia: The Jewish Publication Society of America, 1959, p. 77.

45. *Ibid.*, p. 110.

46. *Ibid.*, pp. 205, 223.

47. *Ibid.,* pp. 394-395.

48. Joseph Dupuis was quoted by Joseph Williams in *Hebrewism of West Africa.* New York: The Dial Press, 1931, p. 65.

49. Num. 36:5-12.

50. Num. 36:12.

51. Lev. 15:19-29.

52. Ex. 28:15-30.

53. *Jewish Encyclopaedia,* Vol. VI, p. 390, subject, "High Priest." For additional information concerning the Ashantee Jews *see:* Joseph Williams' *Hebrewism of West Africa.* New York: The Dial Press, 1931, pp. 24-92.

54. *See:* Allen H. Godbey, *The Lost Tribes a Myth.* Durham, North Carolina: Duke University Press, 1930, p. 244.

55. Deut. 28:65.

56. *See:* Godbey's, *Works.* Durham, North Carolina, 1930, pp. 244, 245.

57. *Ibid.,* p. 256 (see map).

58. The traffic of the slave trade is meant.

59. *See:* Godbey's, *Works.* Durham, North Carolina, 1930, p. 246.

60. The synagogue of Rabbi Matthew is presently located at No. 1 W. 123rd Street, in the Harlem section of New York City.

61. Lam. 1:3.

62. Jer. 30:3, 8, 9, 10.

63. The bones is meant.

64. The expression, "I will open your graves" means: The black Jews will be released from physical and mental slavery.

65. God will cause the black Jews to leave the country of their oppression.

66. Ezek. 37:1-28.

List of Sources

The history of ancient tribes and races in Asia, Africa and Europe:

DENIKER, JOSEPH. *The Races of Mankind.* New York: Charles Scribner's Sons, 1900.

HERODOTUS. *The History of Herodotus.* Translated by George Rawlinson. New York: Tudor Publishing Company, 1928.

JOSEPHUS, FLAVIUS. *The Life and Works of Flavius Josephus.* Translated by William Whiston. Philadelphia and Toronto: The John C. Winston Company, 1957.

RATZEL, FRIEDRICH. *The History of Mankind,* 3rd Vol. translated by A. J. Butler. London and New York: Macmillan and Company, 1898.

RIDPATH, CLARK JOHN. *Universal History,* 16 Vols. New York: The Jones Brothers Publishing Company, 1897.

WENDT, HERBERT. *It Began in Babel.* New York: Dell Publishing Company, 1964.

The relationship among the three religions of Judaism, Christianity and Islam:

FISCHEL, W. J. *The Jews in the Political and Economic Life of Mediaeval Islam.* London: 1937.

GAER, JOSEPH. *How the Great Religions Began.* New York and Toronto: The New American Library, 1956.

GIBB, H. A. R. "Law and Religion in Islam" in *Judaism and Christianity,* III ed. E. I. J. Rosenthal, London: 1938.

GIBBON, EDWARD. *The Decline and Fall of the Roman Empire,* Vol. II. New York: The Modern Library, 1931.

KATCH, A. I. *Judaism in Islam.* New York: 1954. (Commentary on first three Suras of Koran showing Jewish sources.)

ROSENTHAL, I. J. ERWIN. *Judaism and Islam.* London and New York: Thomas Yoseloff, 1961.

The history of Africa including The Sudanic Kingdoms:

BARTH, HEINRICH. *Travels and Discoveries in North and Central Africa,* 3rd Vol. London: Frank Cass and Company, 1965.
BREASTED, JAMES HENRY. *History of the Ancient Egyptians.* New York, 1908.
———. *A History of Egypt.* New York, 1912.
———. *Ancient Records of Egypt.* Chicago: 1927.
DAVIDSON, BASIL. *Africa: History of a Continent.* New York: The Macmillan Company, 1966.
———. *African Kingdoms.* New York: Time, Incorporated, 1966.
———. *The Lost Cities of Africa.* Boston and Toronto: Little, Brown and Company, 1959.
DUBOIS, FELIX. *Timbuctoo the Mysterious.* Translated by Diana White. New York: 1896.
ROGER, J. A. *World's Great Men of Color.* New York: Vol. I, Futuro Press, Inc., 1947.

The histories of the black Jews of Asia, Africa, Spain, and Portugal:

BRUCE, JAMES. *Travels to Discover the Source of the Nile.* Edinburgh: 1804.
COWPER, H. S. *The Hill of the Graces.* London: 1897.
GODBEY, ALLEN H. *The Lost Tribes a Myth.* Durham, N. C.: Duke University Press, 1930.
GRAYZEL, SOLOMON. *A History of the Jews.* 8th ed. Philadelphia: The Jewish Publication Society of America, 1956.
LINDO, HIAM ELIAS. *The History of the Jews of Spain and Portugal.* London: Wertheimer and Company, 1848.
LIVINGSTONE, DAVID. *Travels and Researches in South Africa.* New York, 1859.
ROTH, CECIL. *A History of the Marranos.* Philadelphia: The Jewish Publication Society of America, 1932.
SLOUSCHZ, NAHUM. *Travels in North Africa.* Philadelphia: The Jewish Publication Society of America, 1927.
WILLIAMS, JOSEPH. *Hebrewism of West Africa,* 2nd ed. New York: The Dial Press, 1931.

Other available books by Dr. Rudolph R. Windsor

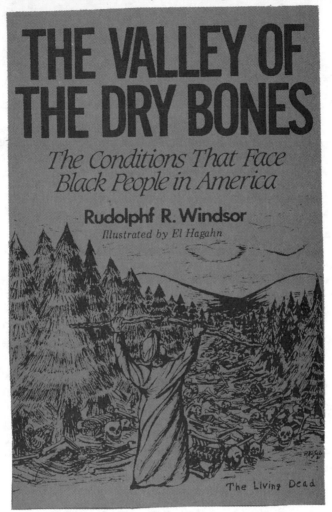

The conditions that face black people in America.

Paperback 162 pages.

For speaking engagements and lectures
write to:
Windsor Golden Series
P.O. Box 310393
Atlanta, GA 31131-0393
email:windsorgs656@gmail.com

ETHIOPIA STILL PLAGUED BY FAMINE: JEWS SUFFER
ETHIOPIAN JEWS MEET WITH SHAMIR

Prime Minister Yitzhak Shamir met last December with members of the Joint Committee for Ethiopian Aliyah who urged that more be done to rescue the 7,000 to 10,000 Jews left behind in Ethiopia.

A recent United Nations Food and Agriculture Organization report predicts that this year, like last, Ethiopia will be the country hardest hit by the African drought and famine. Close to six million Ethiopians are endangered by food shortages.

Gondar Province, home for the 7,000 Jews still in Ethiopia, remains one of the regions most severely affected by the famine. According to the Ethiopian government Relief and Rehabilitation Commission, in Gondar alone, over 300,000 people will need food assistance in the coming year.

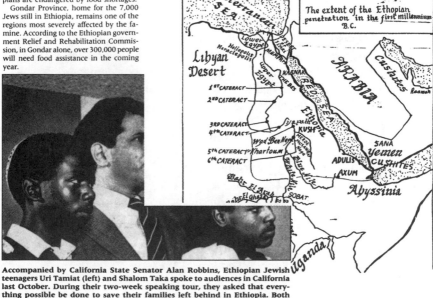

Accompanied by California State Senator Alan Robbins, Ethiopian Jewish teenagers Uri Tamiat (left) and Shalom Taka spoke to audiences in California last October. During their two-week speaking tour, they asked that everything possible be done to save their families left behind in Ethiopia. Both teenagers now live in Israel after being airlifted last year from Sudan. It took them and 120 others almost a year to get to Israel, beginning with a grueling, three-week trek across 700 miles of desert. They spent 10 months in a refugee camp before being rescued.

War, love, and faith are combined masterfully in the retelling of the Old Testament story of Barak and Deborah, two individuals brought together by the hand of God to free their people from the oppressive Canaanites.

Set in 1125 B.C.E., Prince Barak and the beautiful prophetess Deborah form an alliance to rid the land of the scourge of their enemies. In time, the two fall in love with one another—but tradition demands that she marry someone else. Heartbroken that she cannot marry the man of her dreams, she becomes disappointed.

In this magnificent book, there is a special message for our generation that is interwoven within these pages. The Windsors render solutions to the rampant problem of crime in our neighborhoods. They explain in detail, that we can save many of our young men from premature deaths and incarceration by establishing constructive programs. They also believe that this can be accomplished with love, patience, and willpower combined with guidance from strong role models.

For information write to: Windsor Golden Series
P.O Box 310393
Atlanta, GA 31131-0393
Phone: 770-969-1627
Email:windsorgs@comcast.net
Website: www.windsorgoldenseries.com

Price: $17.95 ♦ Paperback 312 pages

Rachel, a young Ethiopian Jew now living in Israel, displays a photograph of her family left behind in Ethiopia. She discovered the photo among ones brought to her school by visitors who had been to her hometown in Ethiopia and had photographed members of the village. Rachel says she likes living in Israel with her sister, but that she is sad much of the time due to the separation from the rest of her family. Currently, some 16,000 Ethiopian Jews live in Israel, but between 7,000 and 10,000 remain in Ethiopia, waiting to be rescued.